32 Houses Later
(A Daughters Tale)

Julie Wansboro

32 HOUSES LATER

ISBN-13:
978-1479174409

32 HOUSES LATER

PART ONE

A daughter, A sibling

Chapter 1

It was May 1981. When I got home from school I found my mum crying, this was unusual, instinctively I gave my mum a big cuddle and ventured the question "what's wrong?" Through sniffs and sobs she replied "Your dad has gone to Northern Ireland, I'm not sure when he'll be back".

This was to be the first time I really understood what 'being in the army' meant for us as a family. Bobby Sands was one of a number of hunger strikers imprisoned in Northern Ireland, my dads regiment was Spearhead battalion which meant they had to deploy to Northern Ireland to cope with the violence surrounding it. I was ten, my birthday was in June, and the first thought that went through my head was 'I wonder if he'll be back for my birthday'. I was oblivious to the fact he might not come back at all, that's how dangerous Northern Ireland was.

I was born in Osnabruck, West Germany on June 29th 1970 second child to Sergeant Kenneth Draycott and wife of Mrs Valerie Draycott in a Frauen Klinik. This in itself was a bit of a problem, I'd not been born in a British Military Hospital so consequently wasn't issued with a British birth certificate immediately, we moved back to the UK when I was about six weeks old (my first flight) to live with my dads parents until a house was ready for us in Oswestry. When my parents came to sort out passports they found my birth had not been registered in the UK, my birth certificate is dated 31st March 1971. We spent about six months at my grandparents in Newport then onto a married quarter in Oswestry. In 1973 we went back to Osnabruck, so by age three I'd already had four homes.

We moved to Northern Ireland and whilst I have little recollection of our first home there I do remember the second house as two events literally scarred me for life. I was at the park aged maybe four, a family friend was supervising, I'd gotten off the see-saw and was stood over the end before another child jumped on the other end, I was hit in the chin splitting it open, I don't remember anything after that, have been informed since that I was carried into the house covered in blood. The scar is quite neat. The second incident that kept that posting in mind was the shed roof. Our house had a sort of linked on shed, it was linked to the porch and had slatted wood on the side. We used to climb up and sit on the roof, only one day Kevin Anderson accidentally stepped on my fingers and I let go, landing face first into stone chippings, got a ride in an ambulance that day. They pulled all the little stones out of my forehead hence a few more scars.

Happier memories of Northern Ireland were my brother Kenny and his friend Vincent Harrhy used to play with Matchbox cars on big long orange plastic race tracks strewn all over our living room. Alan and Helen Harrhy were better known as Uncle Alan and Auntie Helen, Uncle Alan had introduced my parents many years ago in Hereford apparently, they had two children Vincent and Glynn, when Glynn was little he broke his collar bone, I don't recall where we lived but do recall us leaving Glynn in a cardboard box on the sofa as we played, there was a thump and a howl, next thing I know Glynn had a broken collar bone. My mum told me how when my brother was at school one day there was a bomb scare in camp and they weren't allowed to go in and get their children; I couldn't imagine how she felt until many years later.

Our next posting would be to Berlin, oh which is where Glynn Harrhy may have broken his collar bone. Berlin was a divided city; I remember going through the 'Berlin Corridor' to get into the allied forces zone, staring at the guards in their towers around the wall at various intervals, seeing the Brandenburg Gate, climbing the Victory Tower, world war two was a mystery to me back then. My dad was part of a regiment, the Royal Regiment of Wales specifically, he was a Sergeant when my mum married him, the regiment moved as one, like a mobile village, everyone knew everyone, no matter where we went in the world we were together. I knew other kids from the regiment and would meet up with them again over the years. There was a hierarchy too which completely went over my head, although I did know my dad was block senior in Berlin, I had no idea what that meant.

We lived in a ground floor flat and had a budgie named Pippy. My dad used to lift us over the balcony to let us loose in the park. I used to look up at the sky fearful that the flats were moving and about to fall down. The swings were a fierce source of competition, the higher you could swing the greater the status, we'd go higher and higher and jump off, it was a basic park but was enjoyed by all. I was bullied briefly by an older girl who had decided she wanted to beat me up, I ran to the balcony to tell my dad who lifted me over and said "go and hit her first you'll be fine", popping me back down I stood there a bit stunned and thought 'I can do this'. I went back over to the park told my big brother who then told said girl to leave his sister alone.

We had many adventures around the towering blocks of flats. Two of my mums sisters and their children came to stay, I remember the night they all went out and left us with our regular baby sitter, I was vaguely aware of a place called the 'mess' by then. My four cousins went wild, literally trashed the place, one had found the passports and decided to doodle all over them, one had decided to half eat all the fruit in the flat, leaving bits of it everywhere. My brother managed to put the shower on in the bathroom and couldn't switch it off, in short it was bedlam. Then there was the time our budgie died and my mum had to tell my dad at work who, bless him, asked a friend who was able to get away from work to get another one for us so we'd never know. Slight problem the friend hadn't seen our blue long tailed budgie and suddenly Pippy was short tailed and green. Pippy used to live in my dads inside jacket pocket as far as Glynn Harrhy was concerned and he used to talk to Pippy in there. Over the years it became clearer and clearer to me that my parents loved kids and I often wondered why there was just me and Kenny. Went to school for the first time in Berlin, we were bussed to and from school and each bus had names like 'the flower' bus or 'teddy bear' bus. It was easier for us to identify with the picture so we got the right bus home. Personally I think this was a flawed system and relied on my bus escort to go through her list and wait for my name. Handstands against the wall showing your knickers to the world with no worries at all, life is great when you're five.

We were heading back to the UK. To South Wales; the houses weren't quite ready so we went to stay with my grandparents in Hereford for a while. The school in Hunterton was awful, I was bullied from the first day because they decided I was German and didn't belong there, I was too little to understand it but was so relieved when we left and went to the Uplands in Brecon, although that was a short lived house too. Brecon, Christmas 1976, my favourite uncle and family had come to visit, one of his sons managed to smash my dolls bunk bed

7

which I'd had that Christmas, I was so angry. Uncle Trefor had polio meningitis at about eight/nine, he ended deaf but obviously could speak, he learnt sign language and to lip read. I loved him to bits; big bear of a man, his wife was born deaf so couldn't speak so complaining bitterly to either of them about my broken bunk bed was difficult.

Eventually we joined the regiment in quarters in Crickhowell. Again a bus to school and began learning Welsh at school, to this day I can still count from one to whatever. My mum got a job in Crickhowell, later I found out it was as a kitchen assistant in the Naafi, it was short lived as my brother and I couldn't 'behave'. Example being, we fought over a stick in the hallway of the house and I let go, he fell against the corner of the wall (metal strip running down it under the paint), split his head open. We regularly fought as siblings it's what we did. Although I knew when to stop which was usually before either parent intervened, Kenny however used to push it and get told off quite regularly because he had to argue the point. A story Kenny would always tell was that of the glass of spilt milk, I'd spilt the milk but before I could open my mouth and tell anyone he'd said something about it being spilt as he was so pleased I'd done something 'naughty'. In his haste to split on me the information was misinterpreted and he ended up getting a smacked backside as he was shouting over the question he was asked and arguing, was incredibly funny as I did try and confess to the accident. We used to all go out on our bikes and ride around the block as it were, was a huge oval of an estate so the road went all around it, it was great fun. I managed to come off my bike and have all the other cyclists land on top of me, the pedal of my bike was stuck in my knee, eeewww and Crickhowell was the place I did a cartwheel and my hand went into dog pooh!!! I can't decide which is worse!!

Crickhowell was also about going up the Sugar Loaf, visiting my grandparents in Hereford and getting to see all my cousins we had a good life in Crickhowell. I went round the path on my bike alone one day, I met a friend of my brothers who in her infinite wisdom was really friendly for about ten seconds then hit me with a 'whipping' stick, you know the ones, the long thin bendy sticks that sting like mad, she must have hit me three or four times. I went home to my mum, who promptly took me to her parents and showed them my back; the other mum shrugged it off and didn't appear to do anything about it at all. The girl told me it was because my brother had ignored her. I had a good friend in Cathy Iles who lived across the road from us, man she had such a paddy one day, kicked in the a glass panel on the side of the front door at her house, I never did find out why.

Right from the start we had two holidays a year, one with my grandparents in the UK and another in the area we lived, either camping or Butlins. When living close to my grandparents in Crickhowell we used to go and see them quite a lot. Their home became a sort of base, a centre point to our roving lifestyle. My granddad used to work shifts and it always made me laugh that when all the grandchildren were running round like lunatics and playing in the cupboard under the stairs all available adults used to shush us and make more noise than we were! My Nan used to bake and cook seemingly all the time, we all used to get a chance to get in the tiny kitchen and help in some shape way or form. Granddad made wine, it used to ferment in big demijohns in the little bedroom, popping and belching in the night causing raucous laughter. On a Sunday if we were there for a feast of a roast dinner followed by home made rice pudding we'd get the smallest thimble sized glass of Granddads wine.

My grandparents' home was about going for long walks over the fields, Nans' famous Sunday roast dinners, all our cousins and their parents, it was a proper family home bursting at the seams with people on a number of occasions. One Christmas we slept in the living room and I swear there must have been six clocks ticking at various speeds, it was a constant lulling tick-tocking. Valerie Marjorie Wheeler, my mum, daughter number one of four born in Newtown, mid-Wales to Richard Derek Wheeler and Marjorie Wheeler. Auntie Pauline married to Uncle Sam, Auntie Barbara married to Uncle Alan, Auntie Marion married to Uncle Martin, there were sort of two waves of grandchildren for my grandparents', first lot Kenny, myself, Mathew and Simon, Michael and Jimmy, second lot Sarah, Stefan, Amy and Martin. Whilst growing up I was the only granddaughter it was great even if I do say so myself; Sarah having moved to Australia when about 18 months old and Amy never really seeing her grandparents.

Kenneth Francis Draycott, eldest son of 'our Lofty' and Kenneth Francis Draycott, then Uncle Ned married to Auntie Gayle, Uncle Trefor married to Auntie Pat, Uncle Tony, Auntie Gayle married to Uncle Jimmy and Auntie Lynne. Cousins let me see, Stephen and Amanda, Dean, Carl and Mark, Kissan, Adam, Sophie, Haroon and Soraya, Becky and Joy. Our Lofty died when I was not much older than a year old I have no recollection at all of her sadly, my paternal grandfather died when my dad was little and Lofty had remarried. I knew my gankie, I have no idea why gankie was called gankie but he was. We visited gankie and Uncle Tony in their house in Newport, South Wales. Gankies' roast dinners were not the same as my Nans' in Hereford but they were made with the same amount of love. Going to see Uncle Ned was always an adventure, the stories told made him appear like a master criminal, I'm sure he wasn't really, one story often told was that of the time he 'found' a whole load of money on the post office counter and decided to play Robin Hood and gave it to as many passing pensioners as he could before being arrested, I wonder if any of them came back to hand it in. We'd see dads' side of the family whenever we stayed at my grandparents in Hereford on day trips here and there. Always the welcome was warm and loving but it seemed a lot of the time when out of sight we were out of mind. It was us four a family unit against the world, living and travelling together.

August 16th 1977 my brother came charging out of the living room and into the kitchen shouting to my mum "Elvis is dead". My mum didn't believe him and came in and sat watching the news totally dumb struck. She loved Elvis along with every other fan I remember watching some of his films with her. There was always music in our house, especially in the car on journeys. Everything from country and western to the latest chart toppers, my dad was always singing too, it's sort of rubbed off on me and my eldest son, my mum just says we're noisy.

Army houses came with army furniture, everything from bathroom stools to wardrobes, sofas to dining tables. We had army cots and then beds, for some unknown reason in my infinite wisdom I gnawed a hole into my headboard whilst in Crickhowell, I walked downstairs and told my parents to tell me off now and was crying, I'd damaged military property and was vaguely aware that it was wrong.

The houses were so new they didn't even have street names; we lived in Number 53 MSQ, married soldiers' quarter. Whilst we lived in Crickhowell my parents bought a three piece suite it was leather with buttons in it, I always remember twiddling with them and my mum being very aware of children with buckles on their shoes.

Chapter 2

Our next move was to be Aldershot however there weren't enough quarters in Aldershot for our large family regiment so some of us were housed in Church Crookham, Hampshire. A four bed roomed end of terrace brand new house, a good sized garden and a parking space out front; it was September 1978, I was eight and this was my 11th home.

I went to the local primary school, a walk away with a long line of parents and children snaking their way there. I didn't feel any different to any other child, we all went to school, we all had milk in little bottles, we all stood and parroted our times tables. I met Chloe Williams, who went on to be a life long friend. She really liked one or our classmates in our final year of primary school Mathew Butcher, dark haired and glasses. Church Crookham was all about long hot summer days, playing in corn fields, going to the pub garden for lemonade and a bag of crisps, swing parks, adventures in and around the estate. Someone came up to me in school one day and said "you get all your food free", I was confused, knowing we went to the supermarket every Saturday the same as everyone else. I asked my dad, he said "we pay rent, tax, national insurance, normal utility bills; we buy our food the same as everyone else".

I felt settled in Church Crookham, I had friends, even a Canadian pen-pal named Camille Langford for a while, life seemed perfectly normal. In no particular order, I met and spoke to Prince Charles whilst living there, he came to the 'mess' during a families day, still makes me laugh to this day, he turned round to this really tall punk with a Mohican and asked "and what is your favourite subject at school?" and in a perfectly upper class rounded accent the lad turned round and said "I enjoy maths and physics". The Sergeants and Warrant Officers Mess, a mess is the place where military personnel

11

socialise, eat, and (in some cases) live, there is also a Corporals Mess and an Officers Mess. My dad was a WO2 so a member of the Sgts & WOs Mess, he'd become such in 1974 aged 29. This Mess was the only Mess I'd known and only knew it as a fun place to go for curry lunches on a Sunday and family days. My parents used to go to the 'mess' for nights out, my mum in long dresses, my dad in a bright red jacket with various badges and medals, they both always looked very smart. Years later on a British Forces television advert about alcohol awareness it shows a mess members clothes strewn all the way up the stairs after a night out and his son kicking the football alone whilst his dad was sleeping off the drink. Soldiers work hard and play hard.

Butlins, Clacton-on-Sea was an awesome holiday, I learnt to swim, my dad had promised 20p per width, took me into the deep end and promptly let me go (clearly he was in rescue me distance), I swam and instantly discovered I love the water, my dad paid up about £2 that holiday I do believe. Kenny spent his pocket money for the whole holiday in one day on a card machine playing higher, lower, based on the television show Play Your Cards Right with Bruce Forsyth. He kept waiting and hoping for that big pay out, it didn't happen.

Weston Super Mare, Clacton and Brighton were the scenes of many clashes between mods and rockers during the 1980s. My grandparents had come with us to Weston Super Mare and there were mods and rockers stood at either end of a long street all crowding together, the mods in their long dark green parkers with union jack targets on the back, the rockers looking like throw backs from the sixties. I gripped my dads' hand tightly sensing the raw aggression in the air, very glad to get home that day.

The Windmill pub at the end of the lane, I say the end of the lane it was like a good two mile walk. Family friends Uncle Gary and Auntie Barbara Gibbs and their children Sian and Dean used to come with us or us with them whichever way you look at it. We used to all play badminton next to our house and then just go for long walks; the good part being the pub was at the end of it. I got my own television for my bedroom and managed to frighten myself by watching Tales of the Unexpected and such on a weekend when my parents would go out to the pub. Of course I was told the tele should be off by whatever time, it never was. An episode was to haunt me for life! A train was going through a tunnel and when a woman looked out of the window a bloodied face was pressed up against it illuminate almost by the blackness around it, she screamed and ever since I've not been able to close the curtains with the lights on inside and it's dark outside. I'm not mad keen on tunnels either!!!

Long hot summers between 1976 and 1982 whilst we'd been in the UK were not a figment of my imagination, I've checked, however, the year we'd gone camping in Cornwall (1978) was one of the wettest summers on record and Uncle Trefors' bubble pop up tent had blown away in a gale, with torrential rain for a couple of days too!! During the six week summer holidays we used to go out and play until the sun went down, we went miles away into the cornfields. We had trips to Southsea with its pebble beaches and hover craft. Uncle Gary and Auntie Barbara came with us to Brightons' nudist beach not long after it opened on 1st April 1980, it was hilarious. Sian and I aged coming up nine and ten respectively were sent off to have a look around, we came back giggling like mad. We'd seen a very wizened black man with everything all shrivelled up and couldn't tell anyone for giggling, eventually I think we managed to say and off our mums went to see what they could see. Everyone was relived that we didn't have to be naked although Sian did declare "I'll go knickerless but not topless".

Uncle Trefor came to Frensham Pond with us, known to us as Frenchmans' Pond or dead fish pond. We went out on Uncle Trefors' blow up dingy/boat thing, I so didn't want to swim in that pond, I'd seen the floating, bloated dead fish, so there we all were on the boat and Uncle Trefor got out and tried to encourage me to get in and swim. I remember hanging off him and trying to keep every part of me out of the water shouting at him "I can't swim", knowing full well he couldn't hear me so I tried to get him to look at me so he could see me, when he did he laughed and said "I know you can" and dropped me in.

I watched my dad being carted off to hospital with gall stones, my parents were having some friends in for drinks but then my dad ended up doubled over in agony which got steadily worse. I don't remember how long he was in hospital for but he told my children and others that the one scar on his side is from a bullet wound and because

Trand and Uncle Ken was a soldier of course they all believed him. There were British Military Hospitals in the UK and abroad then, my dad was taken to the one in Aldershot, the system worked well as servicemen and families all being mobile never had to go on waiting lists for operations minor or major as they weren't part of the civilian system. We had medical centres with our own doctors too and dentists. Cambridge Military Hospital (1779-1996), Aldershot me with stomach ache once and staying overnight.

I met Liz Fraser and had my picture taken with her, got ignored by Joanna Lumley and never forgave her, they were at a family day raising awareness for something or other, when asked Liz Fraser was lovely she came over and stood for the photo but the other one, well the press were in front of her not where we were! We lived next to a Ghurkha camp, John Gleese was in a film that was having some scenes shot in the camp, we all piled around the back gate to try and meet them, which we did; he was so tall. We used to go over to the Ghurkhas mess, it was really good fun. I was given a little Ghurkha kukri broach by friends of the family. They are lovely people, the smell of spice always reminds of them. Got a cracking outfit from Canada after my dad had a tour there, I got my ears pierced, watched Star Wars in a smoke filled cinema, watched Grease and spent most Sunday evenings recording my favourite music from the weeks charts on my radio cassette player.

Music was to become a big part of my life having got my first means of recording it. I think from about aged six I'd remember words to the songs and sing along to the likes of Abba and Kikki Dee, had a thing for Showaddywaddy. Don't Cry for me Argentina sung by Julie Convington was a favourite and I doggedly tried to learn all the words by taping it and rewinding it and playing it again. This was a much used and well loved method for later learning the words to Vienna by Ultravox, Stand and Deliver by Adam and the Ants, Angelo by Brotherhood of Man. I loved Kate Bush and loudly sang along to all of her songs, Wuthering Heights being number one in March of 1978. Each move or 'posting' was to be punctuated by various favourite songs. Each summer having particular memories associated with a song, summer of 1978 was You're the one that I want – Oliva Netwon-John and John Travolta, EVERYONE knew the dance to it. There was

14

a film called Watershipdown that came out that year too and the song Bright Eyes – Art Garfunkel, it had thousands of children in tears, me included.

It was in Church Crookham that my brother went to boarding school, he was disruptive at home and hated school, it was discussed and decided he would be happier settled in one place and school rather than keep moving. There was a television programme on in 1980 called To Serve Them All My Days, it featured a boarding school and it's whole setting was much like that of my brothers school. I remember iron bedsteads with over stuffed duvets and huge imposing staircases. Kenny used to have tuck boxes of goodies sent to him by my Nan who used to bake for Britain and NATO combined I think, which was great, he always had enough to share with his friend Karl Nappit. Kennys' friends were often slightly younger than him or lacking in confidence, he somehow managed to make them shine and come out of themselves. We had Nappit to stay one weekend and they'd a tent out in the garden, they'd sat up all night telling ghost stories and then there was an almighty thumping on the backdoor, it was Kenny, Nappit had gone to sleep just fine and he was sat there hearing every bump, squeak and was worried sick. My dad had to carry Nappit in sleeping bag into the house. We went to a sports day at the school and I remember the 'death' slide it was awesome, I so wanted to have a go but had no idea who I should ask and didn't want to fuss. The candle light carol concert at Christmas, it was just amazing could have brought the hardest of hearts to tears, my mum chokes up at Silent Night. Kenny hated being away from home and lasted all of one school year before coming home.

Margaret Thatcher became the first woman Prime Minister on May 4th 1979, my parents' 11th wedding anniversary. Aged eight almost nine at the time so this meant absolutely nothing to me; though she went on to stay Prime Minister until 1990 so just over half of my childhood.

Power cuts were not uncommon and my parents had gone to pick my brother up from school, there was thick snow and ice, I was staying at Dale and Kimberly Turners house. There was a phone call and my parents had left the road sliding off on black ice and landing firmly between two trees, with the weather being so bad they had to

15

stay in a nearby hotel overnight so I got to stay at the Turners. It was bath night the next thing you know the power had gone so I ended up having my first ever candle lit bath. Had my first 'proper frenchie', was a lad named Nick Stevens he lived next door, we were 'going out', sat behind the houses by his back gate, strawberry blonde with freckles, he wasn't much older than me, first kiss was Dale Turner in the cornfield but that was as they say 'no tongues'.

Last year in primary school and seemingly my parents consented to my having the wonderful sex education lessons. Mr Price all of us thought he was so handsome it's amazing how wrong you are when you're young. All of us sat in the hall sat around a tiny television watching a video, this must have been such a relief to so many teachers all over the world the invention of the Video Home System (better known as VHS) is a way of recording analog television and playing recorded analog videotape based cassette standard developed by Victor Company of Japan (JVC). They no longer had to rely on standing up and explaining it all they popped the video with shadow characters making a baby. Mr Price was clearly seeing one of the other teachers as the pair kept glancing at each and blushing. The mechanics of sex was explained but none of the morals or emotions that come with it.

That year also saw a residential trip to Stubbington. I'd never been away from home and was a bit reluctant. It turned out we were in a long dormitory in bunk beds, we learnt all about flotsam and jetsam, shell's seaweed and the like. There was an inter-dormitory putting competition which I won and was duly rewarded with a chocolate bar from the on site tuck shop.

Tainted Love – Soft Cell the tune of September 1981; I was to go to Courtmoor Secondary School, I had to go via double decker bus. My mum duly gave me bus fare and lunch money every morning and off we went in a group. We could actually jump off the bus at an earlier stop go to the shop buy a bag of sweets and walk the rest of the way to school and still be there on time. Nobody knew my dad was in the army at Courtmoor I was just one of the new first years, however I was already 5ft 6in so nobody really treated me like one. Our head of year was Mrs Lunghi, she used to wear like tweed skirts that looked like carpets, we were all done for water fighting and threatened with the cane thankfully some of us were taken pity on and just got litter duty instead. Rhona Moffet and I went out of school at lunchtime to dog walk, we ended up in the shop and she told me to take a bar of chocolate, I'd said "I've no money" she replied "just take it". Stupidly I did and the very next day was called into Mrs Lunghis' office. It was a case of 'you tell your parents or I will'. I went home and told my mum, she went ballistic and smacked my backside like there was no tomorrow. I was very very ashamed. Think it's the only time my mum has ever smacked me. Anna-Marie Chitty lived behind the school in a bungalow. Her family had absolutely nothing to do with the military and was great to hang out with. She went to France on holiday and brought me back some pencils with little wooden dolls on strings attached to the top and some plastic shells with hard boiled sweets stuck into them. I found the same sweets in a corner shop near my gankies' house coincidentally.

I'm not sure why or when but as a family we had a trip to Windsor and London, I bought a double decker London bus, we visited Madame Tussards, with one of the two schools I attended in Church Crookham I visited the Natural History and Science Museums in London too. Along with a trip to Stratford-upon-Avon to see the Royal Shakespear Company perform A Midsummer Nights Dream, it was utterly amazing even if totally confusing to me. The stage had a mirrored floor, we looked around Stratford too seeing Ann Hathaways cottage.

On July 29th 1981 we all watched spellbound as Lady Diana Spencer married Prince Charles Windsor Prince of Wales (Colonel in Chief of the Royal Regiment of Wales). It had been a fairy tale romance and wedding the whole country celebrated with street parties and coins minted, mugs made, it was a much needed boost to the general public feeling. Princess Diana was shy, pretty and everyone found her magical a true fairy princess the stuff of Disney stories.

The regiment were due to go to Lemgo, West Germany; my dad didn't get RSM so we were posted out to Cyprus. The Falkland Islands some group of islands in the middle of nowhere that most people including me in the UK had never heard of had been invaded by the Argentines in 1982, the islands are British so off soldiers were deployed to defend our citizens. The Royal Regiment of Wales did not form part of the task force sent to deal with the conflict. Having witnessed my dad dispatched at short notice to Northern Ireland I was very relieved that he was not going to 'war' in the Falklands. On the 8 June 1982 while preparing to unload soldiers from the Welsh Guards in Port Pleasant, off Fitzroy, the Sir Galahad was attacked and hit by two or three bombs and set alight. A total of 48 soldiers and seamen were killed in the explosions and subsequent fire.

Back in the day when you moved house you were issued flat pack wooden MFO boxes and screws, each box had six screws on the long side and four on the short sides, total of what forty screws? This time I was old enough to help screw up the boxes; it was amazing even if I did end up with blisters and muscles.

Chapter 3

House number 12 and oddly enough I was 12. A white semi-detached three bed roomed house on an estate outside of camp overlooking Happy Valley on one side and Tunnel beach on the other with a circle of walled bondu/garden in the middle; there was what we named 'the view point' behind what I think was an electricity building of some sort. It was literally a paved area with a small stone wall around it from which you could see both beaches, if you went down to the right you could walk down the peninsular and onto Happy Valley beach. British Forces Cyprus (BFC) are based in two Areas, the Eastern Sovereign Base and the Western Sovereign Base, the UK retains a military presence on the island in order to keep a strategic location at the eastern end of the Mediterranean for use as a staging point for forces sent to locations in the Middle East and Asia. Episkopi was in the WSBA, my dad was a Warrant Officer Two, as far as we knew this was to be his last posting and then he would leave the army and we would settle in one place. Military houses tended to consist of whatever colour walls the last occupant had painted them and whatever colour carpet the army thought wouldn't go with the army dodgy curtains. Later in life I learnt about 'march ins' and march outs'. We had all decided what our bedrooms would be like, what pets we were having the works.

Cyprus was amazing, the history of the island the whole experience. Aged 13 I performed in Macbeth in Kourions' Greco-Roman theatre better known to us as Curium amphitheatre. There was so much to see and do in Cyprus, I spent a lot of time at the beach or the pool, equally as a family we explored the island, the mountains, the ruins of ancient civilizations, the Queen came over at one point and we all stood along the side of the road to witness her smile and wave as she went past in her car. We went up and saw the dividing UN line near Nicosia; it was a bit of a mystery to me. Seems there had been a conflict and the Turkish had invaded and taken more or less half the island, the Turkish never left so the UN was based there to keep the two sides apart.

The trip up to the Troodos Mountains the first time was hilarious; we were in the heat and warmth of Episkopi one minute and then a good four foot of snow the next. We were freezing but loved the snow. Straight into the nearest well only hotel for hot chocolate and a warm-up, subsequent trips were better organised.

My grandparents came over a few times to visit, my granddad even learnt to swim again one year. We saw all the sights, The Temple of Aphrodite, Sanctuary of Apollo, Kolossi castle (one of the Knights Templers strongholds), Tombs of the Kings which is a UNESCO World Heritage Site, Kourions' Greco-Roman theatre and much much more.

I learnt to ride joining the stables in Happy Valley; it was seriously smelly there with the heat and sweaty horses and horse pooh! We were responsible for all aspects of our horse from cleaning the tack through to mucking out. To the tunes of Girls just wanna have fun – Cyndi Lauper, Nathan Jones – Banarnarama and all the chart hits blasting from British Forces Broadcasting Services (BFBS) we'd dance our way round the tack room cleaning our stuff. Lysander was a beautiful horse with a long lolloping canter but awkward trot, my preferred horse for a long ride. Oberon was a stroppy beggar and I had a nice black and purple toenail which promptly fell off after his stepping back onto my toe!! Kekopas was just funny, he liked to kick though and was stubborn as well a mule! There were polo ponies too, an absolutely stunning stallion named Red Lion, with white socks wasn't keen on having anyone in his stable with him and liked to dance,

I had the privilege of being allowed to ride him once or twice, he was way too strong for me but I loved him anyway.

Youth Club, located inside camp but only a walk away was a must. It was literally a porter cabin but everyone used to go there. Tracey Shearing was my closest friend, she lived on camp and her mum and dad smoked! Traceys' dad was a Corporal; I didn't really know or care what that meant we were best friends and shared everything including boyfriends. Whilst sat in her bedroom feet rested on her windowsill she shaved one of my legs, I was fuming, I've had to shave them both ever since! We were sat in her dining room one day and she asked if I smoked, being a bit naïve and not having known her that long I said yes. She inadvertently gave me my first cigarette. It was cheap and everyone did it, like drinking, if you could get someone to buy the cigarettes and alcohol or someone had it that's what you did. It was a far cry from the innocent naïve 12 year old that had arrived on the island!

Andrew Smith one of my brothers friends was a somewhat shy and quiet lad; we had a snog behind the youth club. Neither of us ever told anyone well until now, sorry Andrew. Kenny, Andrew et al were really into heavy metal music, a group became known as the Epi Headbangers, I sort of attached myself to them and joined in the with the head banging, seriously not good, hurts your neck and everything. People used to bring records back from the UK; it was great we'd get the latest top forty. The school used to hold inter-school sporting events in Happy Valley and it was at one such event I bumped into Mathew Butcher, he hadn't changed a single bit.

They had this thing called the Happy Valley Hill climb. Not sure how long we'd been in Cyprus but it was a matter of weeks rather than months and I decided to do it, I ran nearly the whole thing and was so proud when I received my certificate. I always thought I'd do it every year we lived there but that was to be the one and only time. I learnt to type in Cyprus, in an after school club on a big klunky old fashioned type writer. We were bused to school in hot cramped uncomfortable buses driven by locals; who were nutters, I'm glad it was a short distance! St Johns was a very modern school with an outdoor stone amphi theatre and swimming pool. Classrooms were large and airy over two storeys with lots of open courtyards.

I enjoyed History, Geography, English and French at St Johns, also Religious Education. Our RE teacher taught us about every single solitary religion under the sun from Moonies through to Buddhist monks and in a way that was completely engaging and fascinating. I had two full school years at St Johns, completing my 2nd and 3rd year, at the end of the 3rd year we took end of year exams the results would have helped with taking our 'options' for our exam years. During one such exam whilst minding my own business I had to excuse myself and go to the toilet, oh what joy I'd become 'a woman'! If for whatever reason you were as I unprepared for this to happen at school you could go to the nurse and purchase a sanitary item, unfortunately that particular day I had spent all my money at the tuck shop. I vowed to pay it before my name came over the tannoy the next day as EVERYONE knew why girls were asked to go to the nurse over the tannoy. I got home taking Tracey with me determined not to mention the days happening and Tracey told my mum, who shouted upstairs "oh you're a woman now". I have never understood why this is celebrated. Clutching the coin the next day my first stop was the nurses office to avoid any further shame.

The beach, usually we'd all go to Happy Valley beach, by all I don't mean my family. It was always a gang of us 'teens'. Some muppets would jump off the cliff, I stuck to the odd jump of the big rock up one end of the beach, without sounding ungrateful there was only so much sun, sea and sand you could take so it really was all about the company and the music. The pool was home to much fun, one of the life guards English wasn't very good at all and he'd spotted something floating in the water and explosively shouted "someone has shit in my pool, who is shit in my pool?" Many a parent was covering small childrens ears and throwing disdainful looks, us teens were rolling round the floor laughing having leapt from the pool at the first shout. There was a place to get hot snacks, it had a Pac Man video game machine in there too, lunch at the pool would consist of one hot sausage roll with brown sauce, a drink and sitting on the stool playing Pac Man. It brings to mind a phrase now well used in our house and for years to come "this is the life what more could you ask for?"

Our neighbours' were Fred and Sheila Davies, Sheila was pretty much deaf but we managed to get on alright. Kenny and me came home from school to see a snake making it's way down the path so we went in and told my mum (serious snake phobia) who promptly sent me next door to tell Sheila to shut her doors, whilst I was round there mum duly shut every window and door of our house. Sheila was either having a snooze or couldn't hear me, so I went in through her front patio doors to tell her and back out to go home.......I couldn't get in, no matter how much I shouted for my mum to open a door she couldn't hear me! The snake wandered off to wherever unwanted snakes go and eventually after convincing my mum said snake was gone and banging on the front door hammer and tong I was allowed in. Their son was in the UK at college or university he came over with a friend of his one summer. The friend was a tallish skinny lad, bit of a geek looking, but really friendly and incredibly nice, we sat on my parents kitchen table chatting for hours one evening, afterwards he asked how old I was, I replied 14 to which his jaw dropped and he was having none of it, marched into the living room and double checked with my parents. He was quite upset, seems he was thinking of asking me out, apparently 'love struck' Sheila confided to my mum at a later date.

Music was hard to come by in Cyprus and I was so pleased when I was sent Now That's What I Call Music on two cassettes that he'd recorded from his albums'. BFBS was great for keeping us up-to-date with the latest and greatest chart music, it was even better if someone brought the latest records to youth club. I was so pleased to receive the cassettes. Music blasted from my bedroom once more. After various babysitting jobs and pocket money I'd saved enough money to buy myself a Walkman personal portable radio cassette player, it was brilliant being able to play my cassettes whenever and wherever I wanted to. Cliff Richards had a song with the words 'wired for sound' in and 'bobbing along with her head full of music', it fitted these devices perfectly.

BFBS radio was also great for the competitions to win crates of beer or tickets to dinner etc. One of our family favourates was twenty-one questions, each contestant would ring in and ask two questions and receive yes or no answers. We won a few times and merrily received some crates of Carlsberg. Keo was the islands local brewery, Keo brandy being a firm favourate. There was a wine festival held in Limassol every year, my parents went one year and you grab yourself some plastic cups and or a demijohn at the start and go round and taste all the wine.

In the bondu/garden bit of our estate there were held the occasional bbq. After one such bbq my brother had gone out to 'help' tidy up the following morning. There was a knock on the door and his friend was there saying my parents had to go outside quick. My brother had been mine sweeping all the nearly finished bottles and demijohns of all the alcohol that was left outside. I have no idea what happened as I was on my way out but from what I was subsequently told he was very very sick and made good friends with the big white telephone talking to God.

My dads Auntie and uncle came over to see us in Cyprus. Great Uncle Ron and Great Auntie Dot, Uncle Ron liked a wee drink, Auntie Dot liked a wee drink but was mindful of how much of a wee drink Uncle Ron would have. It was really funny listening to the conversations while laying in bed late into the night as my mum was instructed on the size of drink Uncle Ron was to have and when, then hearing Uncle Ron chuckling and changing the drinks order somewhat. I remember Auntie Dot as being a bigger imposing lady; she had worked secretarial all her life and a member of the Womens Institute amongst other various groups. She scared me a bit.

My brother had quite an explosive temper, when in a rage a lot of what he said was hurtful but later you found out that whilst it was hurtful what he had said was the truth as he saw it. Most of his temper was directed at my parents or me, if things weren't going well at school or with his friends we'd get the brunt of it as he wasn't confrontational outside of home. During our posting in Cyprus it sort of came to a head, my mum took him to the doctors who told her, Kenny was in need of security, not the kind of a close family, he had that, the living in one place and having one set of friends from birth to death type security, there was nothing other than insecurity wrong with him. We were all looking forward to that, to settle. The only pets we'd had was the budgie in Berlin, we all wanted a dog or a cat, a rabbit whatever, all of them. We wanted to be near family again, close enough to spend the weekend or a couple of hours. Six years of being able to do that had readied us.

One day I was in the car with my dad, coming back from the library, we were stopped by this man (my fathers Lt. Col) he leant his head into the window and told my dad 'congratulations'. My dad was to be Garrison Sergeant Major to the UN force in the Sinai desert Egypt, a promotion taking him to Warrant Officer One, which was very strange as we were in our last year of the army as far as we all knew. My fathers' response was "Good God Sir". He was to go for six months.

Whilst dad was away in the Sinai Kenny seemed to get worse with his temper, my grandparents came to stay and witnessed one eruption. They were surprised even though my mum had told them about his temper I don't think they'd seen him in full rage until then. My mum never really told my dad how badly Kenny spoke to her or how awful his rages were but then she never told anyone. My parents were proper parents, they both took responsibility for taking care of their children but obviously my dad went away, not just on operational tours of duty but training for those tours of duty too, consequently my mum was effectively a single parent at those times. Waving your dad goodbye without really grasping the fact that anything could happen while he's gone was easy enough because you knew your mum would look after you; of course I missed my dad while he was away but the routine of life didn't change. All my friends dads went off on tour or exercise, none of us found it strange. I never really considered how it was for my mum.

We went to visit, a ferry over to Haifa and a trip around the Holy Land in what 12 hours flat. It has stayed with me my whole life. There were women and men in military uniforms holding guns stood at bus stops, the heat was intense. I was left completely spell bound by the whole thing.

The birth place of Jesus Christ, Mount Calvary, The Wailing Wall (or Western Wall), all the things I'd heard about or read was right there, it was a very haunting experience. The way of the cross, we walked down which many pilgrims only dream about being able to do. One of our guides believe it or not was a deaf mute, my dad was delighted that he could communicate with him and in fact it was an amazing trip. Seems the guide had never seen a brown eyed blonde, my tanned skin and slim build clearly had nothing to do with his awe struck expression, offered my dad some camels for me apparently, but isn't that a story everyone tells after a trip?

Sat in the car again with my dad not long after his return from the Sinai we were once more made to pull over. Another piece of news dropped in through the window, I didn't hear this time but fate saw to it that we were not to have our dreams of black bedrooms and twenty rabbits; my father was to be commissioned. Off to Lemgo, West Germany to rejoin the regiment, my dad as Families Officer, a Lieutenant no less! There I was at 14 returning to a regiment that had all been together since day one and now an officers' daughter to boot.

Chapter 4

A large detached four bed roomed house, with four roomed cellar and concrete floored attic with electricity, right on the edge of the officers patch with other ranks down to the right side of the house at the end of the rather large sloping garden. Home number 13, 15 Buchner Strasse, located not far from the back gate of camp.

First year in Lemgo was a bit of a learning curve, learning to fit into a well established 'village', learning to cope with my dads' new status, after year one things' definitely settled. Year two saw my brother join the army and my friend Chloe coming over to stay, also lots of baby-sitting and various boyfriends, including the first soldier, I have to chuckle at this point. There was a general unwritten law of the gang; you didn't go out with anyone who wasn't one of them. There were 'the boys' and 'the girls', it was stuff of Grease, quite simply you went out with one of the boys you didn't go elsewhere. A small handful had once attempted rebellion and failed, I didn't care, none of 'the boys' had asked me out and this soldier had.

All their friendships had been formed and bonded over the years there were very few 'outsiders', if your dad was in a corps you were posted individually and so many of those children found it hard having to make friends every move. For me returning to a regiment after what was essentially six years away. I was 5 foot 7 inches, I was tanned with long blonde hair, and I wasn't part of the gang. Thankfully the Gibbs were there when we arrived, Sian and Dean as friendly as I remembered. That year we went on holiday to a caravan park at Lake Garda with the Gibbs, it was a memorable holiday. It was some road trip stopping overnight in Austria not far from the crystal factory. We went to Venice, feeding pigeons in St. Marks Square, which was utterly amazing, I had my first and last ever holiday romance, Ilario, he stole my hat and wouldn't give it back, the start of a lovely two week fling, he even took me up to his village on the back of his scooter to meet his parents, I later realised he thought I was a lot older than my 14 years and was planning on asking my parents if he could marry me. Bless him.

Lemgo youth club, either you went to the club and fitted in or you didn't and stood on the outside of the gang looking in. I made the effort, made some friends but always knew I was on the outside, I wasn't like them for some reason, I went to youth club, I hung out on the Pavilion, but my dad was an officer simple.

We under age drank and smoked, most of us didn't do anything to excess, we were all mindful that our dads were in the army, Herforder beer sold in what we called 'yellow handbags' was a popular Friday night buy. You'd buy whatever booze you could get away with buying and because cigarettes were rationed ask someone old enough with a ration card to buy them for you or buy German brands from the many vending machines in the area. Someone always had a cigarette or beer if you wanted either. The girls used to sit in a huddle on the pavilion and discuss how 'far' they'd gone and with who, I'm quite sure the boys did the same. I was always incredibly truthful and compared to some others naïve and inexperienced. It seemed most lads were happy to be my friend just they fancied my friends and didn't ask me out, I used to get messages to give to my friends that they did fancy.

I can't help smiling recalling this meeting. I met Tom Norrington-Davis in Lemgo officers' mess one Sunday not long after we got there. We sat in the bar and Tom put lots of drinks on his dads tab and we smoked unseen by parents who were all in the garden. We became firm friends but he was at boarding school so only ever saw him during the holidays. Julie Vidler moved to Lemgo, we'd been friends in Church Crookham so it was good to be together again, Julie too had been at boarding school but her parents had decided she could do her 'A' levels in Germany. We went to Prince Ruperts School, Rinteln, West Germany. Bused daily there and back with an escort, one week we had to have an armed guard on the bus, whish was weird. I was starting the fourth year and had taken my options. For my brother well he had moved half way through his exam years, we would study over two school years for exams at the end of the second year, he literally did the first part in one school and the second in Prince Ruperts, Kenny found Lemgo difficult, almost like he didn't really fit. It was where we also met up with Kevin Anderson again, first thing I remember saying to him was 'thanks for the scar', the one of my forehead. Chloe Williams from Church Crookham came over and we had an absolute blast, think it was after her visit I gave up bacardi!! Faces from the past all merged together.

In school I was doing History 'O' Level, we learnt all about the Arab/Israeli conflict and also a project about the Berlin Wall and the division of Germany. We went on a trip to Berlin; it was one of the best weeks of my entire life. The artwork on the Berlin Wall was amazing, the guards scary, the trips to the museums and Reichstag fascinating. We took a trip into East Berlin and I remember being told to hold our passports to the window and NOT to turn them past page six or was it sixteen I don't recall but the American children on the trip was a different page so that confuses the memory. (My excuse and I'm sticking to it). All the things I'd taken a great interest in as a younger child were now part of my education and my understanding was vast, I ate the information up and couldn't get enough of it. I took lots of pictures for my project, noting a tribute to Bobby Sands in one mural and wondering why his name should be up there. A lot of things I'd seen and done as a younger child all seemed to have edited together in this one subject.

Everyone it seemed had a nick name when we'd arrived, among these were Milk, Mouse, Neld, Rat, Pea, mine was Spider. Before you ask I have no idea, I went to youth club like week one of being there and the following day I became Spider. It was actually alright for a nick name. BFBS radio was important in Germany too, we only had one television channel which showed as much of the general entertainment as it could so music dominated life, Wham, Duran Duran, Boy George, Eurhythmics, Phil Collins, U2, The Damned, Depeche Mode, Pet Shop Boys, Spandau Ballet, Michael Jackson, Kylie Minogue, Prince to name but a few of the artists dominating the charts. There were Goths, Mods, Punks, New Romantics, so many genres; pop music was taking off with a roll of hits from Stock Aitken and Waterman who from 1984 onward wrote prolifically attaining their first number one with You Spin Me Round – Dead or Alive in March 1985.

Our youth club used to go visit other youth clubs in British Forces Germany, usually for discos but sometimes for sports meets. During one big disco I bumped into Andrew Smith I blushed from head to toe but laughed inside so hard, he'd become a bit of a goth and his girlfriend was all pale and black lipstick. Not the blonde, tanned shy lad I'd known a couple of years before. I played badminton doubles with Adrian Maskelyne at one meet did pretty well too, on the bus on the way there we were all singing along to Walk of Life – Dire Straits. Singing on buses was always a must, on the way to theme parks, school wherever.

Kenny was to join the army, the Welsh Guards and being just 6 foot was quite short for a guardsman, he was part of a company known as 'the little iron men'. After doing his training in Pirbright and our all going over to watch his passing out parade he was posted to Germany specifically Honer, just outside Belson. He came home quite regularly and often with friends. This was a confident happy Kenny, the life suited him and the discipline had improved the control of his temper. His stories from camp were funny though we still fought like siblings do. One weekend he brought two lads home and I'd been minding my own business playing the stereo in the living room when they all piled in, Kenny kept getting up and turning my music off or down and flicking me. In the end I slumped onto the sofa really angry and as he walked past to flick me I punched him full force in the stomach he went down like a sack of shit as the phrase goes. From that day forward his friends in the army thought it was funny to nick name me Rocky, not that it stuck as I already had a nick name!!

28

May 1986 I went to Tracey Jones leaving party in the band room, our school band were going to play which was just fine by me as I was totally in awe of their guitarist Pete, he was a goth, tall, slim and mysterious. That night I ended up going out with Colin a month before my 16th birthday. June 1986 exams done I'd left school with the intention of returning to sixth form to do A levels in English and History. I wasn't able to do my 'A' levels I was an 'O' level short, so I went back to do an NVQ, I stuck it out for a while but hated it so left and started a YTS on camp in the office. I often found myself staring at the clerk in there Jock Anderson, I thought he was yummy but I was 'out with' Colin and Cpl Anderson was engaged as far as I knew. In September of that year my parents had gone away for the weekend leaving me to have the house to myself. I decided on a belated birthday present to myself. By Sunday afternoon I think the entire youth population of Lemgo knew exactly what the present was!!! Colin left to go back to basic training on the Monday so I was left to face the teasing alone, I was not impressed.

In the October Kenny brought Alan John Williams home, Fruitbat, Williams 18, a tall, slim man with an interesting face. It was clear he liked me and I was angry at Colin so was quite happy to start seeing Alan. It was fine, I didn't see him every weekend and we used to write to each other practically daily and the odd phone call here and there. Whilst taking the 'boys' back to camp we decided to go and see Bergen-Belsen, the site of a concentration camp where thousands of people were murdered or left to starve to death. The pictures near the entrance and the general feel to the place was chilling. The Belsen visit put a lot of things into perspective for me, having been to Israel and Berlin previously and following my history 'O' level the experience was compounding. The rumours that no birds flew over Belsen were untrue as far as I could tell that particular day, but the mass graves with the simple wooden plaques with the total number of people in there was chilling to the core.

Music in the car for trips back and forth to UK or Honer was Foster and Allen, Chris de Burgh and if lucky we could persuade my dad one of the Now cassettes. My grandparents visited as did Auntie Dot and Uncle Ron, my parents social life in the Officers Mess was well established and baby sitting was an excellent top up for my rubbish

YTS money. One regular gig was the Naafi Managers baby, I think I first looked after him when he was six weeks old, I watched him grow. Alan came over one night for an hour to sit with me and he lifted the baby up and he threw up on his chest. Babies can be gross.

By Christmas I had decided I didn't want to see Alan anymore, on the advice of Jock Anderson I should get my Christmas presents first and bin him in the New Year. That did make me chuckle but as it turned out I didn't see him before Christmas face to face and at that time didn't have the heart to just bin him on the phone or by letter. My mind had turned to Colin and knew he'd be back for Christmas. Kenny, Alan, my parents and I were all sat in the living room watching anything and nothing and chatting when the doorbell rang, quick as a flash my brother answered the door, there was a short pause and chat at the doorstep and he walked back into the room and said "did you know Julie slept with Colin?". I was mortified and left the house. On my return about two hours later my mother was raving about going over and telling them to stop spreading lies about me. I had to get a hold of my dad and confess to my September belated birthday present to myself.

I thought at this point my parents might have considered that I was sexually mature and active seeing as I was 'out with' a solider and had hoped that a contraception chat may have followed from one of them. No such luck and no amount of conversation manipulation managed to have my mum say "right off to the medical centre and on the pill with you". I even tried the "how did you stop having children after me and Kenny" tact but to no avail. There was no way on this planet I was going to go to the Medical Centre and ask to go on the contraceptive ill aged sixteen and a half, my dad as Families Officer would have known by the 'village' jungle drums by teatime. We relied on luck and condoms. Alan went away in the January so Christmas presents in hand I still wasn't able to 'finish' with him as it seemed cruel to do so while he was away. I wasn't to see him again until mid February, by the end of February I was pregnant.

I did not tell a single living soul, I planned our engagement which as far as people knew was going to be a very long engagement, I'd gone into school and they'd agreed I could go back and do my A levels in the September but then I had a better idea. My parents had been discussing buying a house in Hereford to be close to my grandparents and for me to go to college in the UK. It fitted perfectly in my head, my parents would buy a house, I would get into college, the baby that nobody knew about would go to the college crèche and everything would be fine. I carried on as normal, remained thin, drank, smoked and partied. In July I went to the UK for my college interview which I passed with flying colours and to meet my future in-laws, it was whilst in Abererch I told Alan I was pregnant.

We were engaged officially on July 31st 1987; I was pale and looked ill. I continued to go to youth club and ride roller coasters on the many trips to the various fun parks around Lemgo, Stuckenbrock being one of them. Late August I got out of the bath and my mum was drying my hair, sat on the stool in front of her dressing table she said "you're pregnant aren't you", I said "yes" looking directly into the mirror but avoiding her face. "When are you due?" "November 19th"

I didn't want to stay in Lemgo because I knew exactly what would happen next, there'd be finger pointing and name calling, gossip and nastiness that I just couldn't cope with. I asked if I could 'go to college' as everyone was expecting me to do, it was code for my going to stay at my grandparents to have my baby in peace. My mum came with me to my first doctors appointment I was seven months gone and four pints down on a full blood count, the doctor made it quite clear I could have died on delivery possibly taking my baby with me. Sobering thought at seventeen and three months.

PART TWO

A spouse, A mother

Chapter 5

September 1987 my parents and my mate Julie Vidler, my brother and as many relatives in the UK as we could muster at short notice gathered in Hereford Registry office to witness the marriage of Guardsman Alan John Williams to Miss Julie Anne Draycott daughter of Captain Draycott. My brother sat in the front row his face ashen the whole time. Kenny had tried to split us up a few times since we'd met and then felt responsible for my predicament, he should have known better. The moral upbringing I had dictated that you make your bed you lie in it. Take responsibility for what you do and face up to the consequences.

Life at my grandparents was almost perfect, I no longer worried about my pregnancy and post blood transfusion blossomed. My granddad was like a little mother hen but didn't fuss me only asking on occasion why I wasn't wearing stockings, wasn't I cold. They had bought a microwave, a new fangled gadget that had become popular in the United Sates of America with approximately 25% of the population owning one, it was supposed to make cooking quick and easy, bless his heart my granddad ate every over cooked and rubbish meal I attempted to cook in it. Everything for the baby was bought from babysitting money I'd saved and my pittance of YTS wages. Alan sent virtually nothing even though he knew I had to pay keep (my grandparents were pensioners) and buy things for the baby. 2nd Lieutenant Tate (he of the Tate & Lyle sugar company) came on the phone one evening because his guardsman couldn't cope with his wife in tears on the end of the phone saying she needed more money. A calm voice was telling me that the best was being done and that said guardsman had debts in Germany that I clearly knew nothing about and that we would soon be together in a house in Pirbright, the battalion was posted there. I sucked it up and stretched every penny as far as it could go. My child would want for nothing.

The weekend before baby was due my parents came over, they drove me over every bumpy track they could hoping that maybe baby would arrive a couple of days early. They bought the wheels to go with the carry cot I'd bought, it was soft grey and I'd bought white and lemon big flat sheets then cut them down and sewn them into cot sheets. My Nan had taught me to knit years before and I bought some chunky soft wool and knitted two blankets, my Nan finished them with wide ribbon, they were gorgeous. I was content at my grandparents, I'm not quite sure the reality I would have to move in with my husband at some point had sunk in.

I was no longer Julie Anne Draycott daughter of Captain and Mrs K F Draycott; I was Julie Anne Williams wife of Guardsman A J Williams 18. I was officially a grown up.

My Nan made great chips and the night before my hospital check up the last before my due date I was helping her in the kitchen. She'd left the raw potato chips in cold water ready to cook while the oil heated in the pan. I asked if they were going in as they were without being drained and dried a little, nan said it was fine to just shake and drop them all in. The pan of oil caught fire and quick as a flash my granddad was there with a damp tea towel straight over it. Disaster adverted but I missed out on my chips. When it came to saying goodbye the following morning my granddad gave me a kiss and said see you when I see you. I chuckled and said I'd be back later that morning. He gave me a knowing smile and off Nan and me went for the bus.

I got to the hospital, had my routine appointment and then they told me I had to stay in. I went back to the ward I'd had my blood transfusion in and sat on the bed wondering why. Nan went home and got my hospital bag and as I was expecting to stay overnight off she went home. I'd planned to have the baby alone as my husband was unable to take extended time off on the off chance the baby would arrive on time, clearly had we been in the same country and house this wouldn't have been an issue. I was sat on the bed doing a kriss-cross puzzle book and listening to my personal radio cassette player when I was told my waters were to be broken, so off we went into another room where I sat and watched television and they did their thing, so we all then waited.

David John Williams born Wednesday 18th November 1987 in Hereford County Hospital at 9pm, it was just the midwife and me. China in your hand – T'Pau was the UK number one in the charts and

34

holding my small son for the first time was precious. Our first visitors were my Nan and Auntie Barbara. I was supposed to stay in hospital for five days but Alan had come over from Germany as soon as possible and I left on day three as he only had the weekend. I don't think I've ever seen the look I saw on my grandfathers face before or since when he set eyes on David. It was a mix of so many things in an instant, pride, love, almost a look of total awe, he held him so carefully yet securely and the phrase as pleased as punch springs to mind.

My parents hot footed it from Germany and met their grandson. It made me wonder again why they'd only had two children. Christmas 1987 I went over to Germany, married and with a child, the 'village' knew but didn't know if that makes sense. Jock Anderson the person I'd worked alongside right up until I went couldn't believe the baby was mine and that I was married. In general everyone was lovely and David was spoilt rotten with clothes and presents from all and sundry. My brother absolutely adored his nephew. The idea of leaving my family home and unit for good filled me with utter dread.

I moved to Pirbright in January 1988. My parents and the regiment were still in Germany. The IRA were particularly active a total of 12 British Military personnel were killed by them in that year. Whilst the regiment were moving back to the UK the RSM of the regiment Michael Heakin was shot dead at traffic lights, he was alone in the car, his family were flying back. It was one of the worse things I ever remember. The family lived behind our house in Lemgo, a really lovely family too. The regiment moved to Warminster under a solemn cloud.

I'd moved to Pirbright in a white van driven by Alan. It was a little two bed-roomed brick house, the curtains and carpet were worn and the kitchen ancient. I brightened the kitchen by putting lemon and white sticky back plastic on the surfaces. We didn't have a car and I didn't know any of the wives, I was probably the youngest wife there too at seventeen and a half. Kenny had moved over with the Welsh Guards so was stationed in Pirbright too. I knew various friends of Alans and they came to the house with their girlfriends, which was great as they were much nearer my age. Julie Vidler came to visit and started seeing a lad called Jonah, his nick name, never did find out what his real name was, just knew him as Jonah Jones.

Julie Vidler was staying with us for the very first Red Nose Day in February 1988, we'd gone into Woking and wore our noses all day, even had our photograph taken by the local news paper, never did see the article though. Woking was a walk and train ride away and where I did all of my shopping, pushing David in his pushchair all the shopping in the tray below or hanging off the handles.

I went to Buckingham Palace and stood inside the grounds to watch the changing of the guard, also to Windsor Castle to watch them the Welsh Guards in action. The ceremonies were amazing, full of pomp and glory. I was proud to be Kennys sister with his highly polished boots and perfect bearskin, although the only real bearskins are worn by officers. Alan was a drummer with the corps of drums and whilst his uniform was smart it was different to that of the other Guards. Whilst living so close to London it was worth doing the 'sights'. My cousin Stefan and Auntie Barbara came to stay and off we went on the train, the escalators filled me with horror, they were so steep and narrow. The Natural History Museum was a must and Stefan loved all the skeletons, we walked all over London, seeing Big Ben, The Houses of Parliament, standing outside Number 10 Downing Street, taking in Nelsons Column and so much more, we did the whole thing in a long day and slept soundly that night.

We had an active social life, my 18th birthday party being held in the local Phoenix Club with a disco hired and Chloe Williams being a guest, it was great living so close to her again. She'd learnt to drive and came over on occasion for a chinky, bringing our friend Lisa along too. Lisa used to regularly fall asleep earning the nick name doormouse form me. After the party we'd all come back to our house, it was then I discovered the babysitter was actually thirteen not sixteen as I'd thought. It didn't worry me as I'd been babysitting at that age. I went up to check on David, I'd heard him cry I'd thought. When I picked him and changed his nappy I discovered the babysitter had put it on back-to-front, I laughed to myself and thanked my lucky stars nappy changing hadn't featured largely in my own babysitting experiences.

My closest friend was a German born, Russian lady named Nelly, her son Daniel was roughly the same age as David and we did loads of things together. Her English was hilarious as she'd learnt most of it from her native Welsh speaking husband Stuart. We both had houses full of army furniture including cots for our sons. Christmas 1988 the powers that be decided we were to move into a house around the corner as the one we were in was to be demolished. The carpet was rancid, the curtains not much better and the general state of the 'new' to me house was disrepair. I flatly refused to let David crawl around on the floor and he spent most of the time in his playpen safe.

The company was going on tour to Belize, South America in April 1989. St Davids Day March 1st 1989 after spending most of our married life arguing things came to a head, Alan made to punch me, I ducked, he missed and put a hole in the kitchen door breaking his wrist, there were a number of guests in the house and he left red faced and explosive. On his return after everyone had gone home much much later that night he came with the Families Officer, I was informed that surely he hadn't meant to aim for me and could I have been mistaken. I decided it would be easier to just agree knowing he would be in Belize soon enough.

They eventually came and painted the entire house in colours of my choice, new carpets throughout also my colour choice and curtains throughout, ironically they finished it all as I was intending to leave never to return.

In April 1989 I moved in with my parents in Warminster, back to the Royal Regiment of Wales, the mobile village. At first I'd taken everything I'd need for Alans six month tour of duty but I had no intention of returning when he did. I told my parents just before my nineteenth birthday I was never going back, we went back to the house for the day, I collected everything that belonged to me and any gifts from my side of the family or friends of mine and that was all. I wanted nothing more to do with him. I'd compounded my fate, leaving house number 16 head held high. My only irritant being I had let Alan take my Walkman to Belize with him, I knew I'd never see it again. Ironically it didn't seem a problem to write and end our relationship in print having thought it such a terrible thing to do back in 1986.

I sort a solicitor and started divorce proceedings on the grounds of unreasonable behaviour, he objected to that so it was changed to irreconcilable differences. I went to court in Trowbridge to be told no visiting order was going to be made as he had not applied for one, I stood up and asked what that meant, they said Alan would only be able to see David if he wrote to the court, I said no, he was to have a reasonable access order, I would not be responsible for preventing him seeing his son. I was awarded maintenance for David which I never saw a single penny of, I'd left the joint bank account in credit, returning the cash card and cheque book, I received a letter telling me the account was overdrawn, my solicitor answered it proving I had no access to it, my name was removed from the account.

June 1989, the news was shocking, there had been a peaceful demonstration in China, and it was all over the news as several hundred civilians had been shot dead by the Chinese army in Tiananmen Square (Beijing). I had a far better understanding of the army now, its rank structure and the abbreviations. The idea that an organisation primarily in place to DEFEND its citizens could do that was unthinkable.

Claiming from the state did not occur to me so I looked for a job, several interviews later I started as a data entry clerk at Peter Blacks Toiletries in Trowbridge a walk and train journey away. My mum was to look after David taking him along to crèche and playgroups etc. We agreed keep and life settled into a routine. It was odd the only person who mentioned my return directly was a lady who herself had been divorced and remarried. Tom Norrington-Davies mum, she'd stopped me and lightly said "I hear you've been a naughty girl and left your husband", I laughed and said "yes, not unlike yourself", she changed the subject and mentioned Tom was coming home soon which made me genuinely pleased at the thought of seeing a good friend.

The job was temporary and once it had come to an end I started work in the local camp The Royal School of Signals as an administration assistant for the MOD/civil service, this too was a temporary contract but a walk away from home it meant more time with David. Money in my pocket, a good family life and job life settled into being fun again. My parents loved us being there as much as we loved it. Friday nights down the pub with Julie Vidler, we were in The Bath Arms and they'd started a new cocktails menu, we discovered Black Russians, Tia Maria, Vodka and coke, we could go out with ten pounds and have a great night. I bumped into Jock Forrester, the first soldier I'd gone out with way back in Lemgo; it was good to catch up. He promised to write when I moved to Cheptstow. One of the courses was out and recognised me from work; it was great, don't think Julie or I paid for any drinks!!

Kenny came home from Belize in the September bringing his girlfriend Wendy Flounders with him. They made a great couple and I think all of us hoped she might be 'the one'. The Welsh Guards were still in Pirbright and The Royal Regiment of Wales in Warminster. Kenny had seen his brother-in-law and admonished me for writing a 'dear John', as far as I know he'd read the letter and didn't believe a word of it believing like my soon to be ex-husband that I'd found someone new in Warminster. It hurt to think my brother believed that, though it might have been better to believe that than to think he was responsible for the marriage in the first place or that he hadn't seen the signs of the arguments and general unhappiness.

House count now stood at 17 for me and 4 for David. He enjoyed a great second birthday in Warminster having a train birthday cake and all the neighbours children at his party. A vast difference from his first birthday in Pirbright, when it was my parents, Daniel (Nellys son), my parents and myself.

Chapter 6

My parents were buying a house ready for when my dad might leave the army; we moved into the house in Sedbury just outside Chepstow in the April of 1989, it was the first home my parents had ever owned. The house was end of a terrace row and an ex-army house, the houses across the street were being refurbished and we watched as they received new double glazing and were slowly but surely dragged into the 21st century.

Chepstow has a rich history and the castle is great, but it was a difficult place to live with few jobs, my brother came home to live with us after leaving the army. In November 1989 the Berlin Wall came down, Germany was reunited after three decades of separation. The scenes on the television were amazing. It brought to mind a whole host of memories for a lot of people but the timing had been totally dictated by the people.

My decree nisi had come through in Warminster and I had not realised I was supposed to do anything about it, I got a letter in Sedbury asking if I wanted the divorce to be absolute, if yes I had to go to a solicitor and sign some paperwork and send it back immediately. I then received my decree absolute in the post not long afterwards. Kenny had left the army and had come home to live. David and I shared a bed room and my parents had a blast decorating and furnishing their very own home. I couldn't get a job for love nor money despite several applications there'd been no replies. Kenny and I were statistics, we were on the dole. My granddad said having paid tax and national insurance all his life there was no shame in our taking something back. My dad was of the same mind; as long as we both paid keep and shared the load all would be well. Kenny wasn't great at helping out around the house but then again he didn't make much of a mess either. We both had a good social life going out maybe twice a month, Kenny more often than I as he'd gotten himself a girlfriend and made friends with the local crowd

My parents, David and I had been away for the weekend and upon our return to Sedbury dad bounded up the stairs to tell Kenny we had fish and chips for tea. Kenny came down followed by his girlfriend who my mum greeted happily and asked if she wanted to stay for tea, she declined and hurried off. My dad started laughing and we all just looked at him, he explained he'd caught my brother in the act and said girlfriend had felt my mother had taken the situation very well!! The story was to be retold many times to various friends and family over the years causing much laughter every time.

My choice in music was Erasure and I saw them in concert for the launch of their Wild albumn in 1990. It was fantastic, they sang all the new albumn and then all my old favourates. I bought tickets to see Prince that year too but sadly was unable to go; Prince had been a firm favourate since the release of Purple Rain (1984). I was bitterly disappointed and sold the tickets at Chepstow Sunday Market.

Although we lived in Sedbury it never really felt like home and soon enough came the next posting. Hong Kong. There was much debate as to my future, would David and I stay in Sedbury and take care of my parents house, or if we could let alone would like to go to Hong Kong with them. Kenny was staying put, he wanted to stay settled. I looked into what I could do in Hong Kong and whether it really was feesable for me to go. It turned out that the Civil Secretariat was close to the Civil Service structure in the UK and there were a number of jobs I would be able to apply for. I decided to go; I rang the Welsh Guards and obtained a phone number for my ex. Apparently I'd just missed him, I left a message for him to call back, he didn't. Eventually I spoke to his mum and she gave me an address that my solicitor could use to inform him I was taking David out of the country. At this point he had not seen David since the day he left for Belize in 1989 or paid a penny in maintenance. If he had said no, the courts would have ruled in my favor.

Off we went in July 1990, house number 19 aged 20!! I immediately applied to work for the civil secretariat and in the meantime in the local families Naafi shop working with the chill and frozen foods. I was offered a job for the Royal Hong Kong Police and needed to wait for my vetting to come through. The Naafi earnt a wage whilst I waited so all was good.

Hong Kong was hard in many ways, being so far away from my grandparents and other members of the extended family but also a great experience. Tom Norrington-Davis reappeared in my life there, it was good to see him again and we had a great night out in Stanley. We lived next door to Uncle Alan and Auntie Helen, Glyn would come over to live once he'd finished boarding school. Sara Mountjoy one of 'the girls' from Lemgo days was also in Hong Kong with her parents. I think her nick name had been peahen or Pea for short, I'm sure she'll correct this if she reads it. My brother came over to visit in the January of 1991 (he and Glyn getting up to far too many adventures) and my cousin Dean had joined the regiment and he'd spent Christmas with us, but what a place, the hotels, the buildings, the dragon races, The Tian

Tan Buddha on Lantau island, the amazing hole for the dragon through the hotel at Repulse Bay, the airport, the whole culture amazing. They have a light festival in Hong Kong whereby everyone goes down to the beach and makes circles of candles (light) and celebrate. The fireworks for Chinese New Year were fantastic and one year we went and stood at the harbour side to watch. The Peek Tram was scary as, but a must and we did brave it. There was a theme part called Ocean Park and the views from the cable cars up the side of the well mountain/hill whichever you call them was just breath taking.

It was here in 1990 that I met my husband 24795206 Private Wansboro A R. Minding my own business in a pool with three lads down one end and me up the deep end when as I came up from under the water a tennis ball hit my head, seems this was deliberate. I climbed out of the pool and went over to my stuff, drying my hands to take out a cigarette, quick as a flash all three were there, first asking for a spare cigarette, then a light, I quipped "you'll want me to smoke all four next!" Ceic, Pat and Roge all asked if I got free stuff from the Naafi and were disappointed when the answer was no, just discounted if the food had defrosted and needed to be sold immediately. They all vowed to be in the shop the following day for a sausage roll. It turned out that I was to see Ceic and Roge that very night.

Sara and I had decided to go for a drink in Stanley, catching the bus at the entrance to camp we wandered into The Smugglers Inn. My dad had been out to Hong Kong in the 1960s' and was full of stories about Wanchai or 'the Wanch'. It was pretty much the 'red light' district back in the day, however Sara and I were just going for a quiet drink and had no intentions of going into Central or the Wanch. I approached the bar to get our drinks and they appeared beside me and joined us at our table, I introduced them to Sara having let them pay for our drinks (I'm not totally stupid). We all chatted but after a while Sara and I made a move, we had after all decided to stay clear of men!! We went a couple of pubs down to The Lord Stanleys, it was packed and the concertina glass doors were fully open, we went in and managed to get drinks in plastic cups to go sit out on the steps leading down to the beach. When it was my round I was tapped on the shoulder to find Roge shouting in my ear (it was noisy) "I thought you were down the wanch?" Quite clearly I was in front of him so had to laugh and say "no we're sat out the front". He duly followed us out and I was met with the sight of Sara snogging some bloke at the top of the steps, I put her drink near her feet on the bit of wall and went down the steps a bit Roge in tow.

My vetting interview letter arrived, I had to go to some offices for a face to face conversation with a complete stranger, it was somewhat unnerving. Hushed into a waiting room there were two or three of us sat waiting shifting in our seats clearly uncomfortable. "Do you have a partner?" "Have you had a same sex relationship?" just two of the more embarrassing questions asked. The long and short of the purpose to all of this was to see at what price we could be blackmailed with any information that we didn't want as public knowledge. I found myself lacking in anything to tell. I came out of the interview feeling pretty pure and innocent.

Roge met David a couple of days after my meeting him, I was disconcerted by this, obviously I had told him about David and as I was known as Captain Draycotts' daughter if he didn't already know it was common knowledge and no secret. They got on really well but I was worried and told him I didn't want to see him again. To add insult to injury it turned out he wasn't Welsh and his name was Alan! He wrote me the most amazing letter which was delivered by his friend to the Naafi, I sent a message back saying to be at my house for 7 o'clock if you want to go out. He duly appeared.

We got engaged on my 21st birthday, with him dropping to one knee at my party in The Smugglers to much applause. Oh dear lord, my hen night!! Debbie Allen my closest friend in Hong Kong was my last lady standing and we headed into the 'Wanch'. It was a great night, I managed to twist my ankle at the beginning of the night and I hadn't even had an alcoholic drink at that point. Before we'd gone into town we visited the Regimental goat 'Taffy'. The goat came from the Royal Herd and was the Regimental mascot. Debs found him to be totally amiable as he tried to chew at her top.

Alan was an Erasure and a Prince fan, one of the women over the flats was obsessed with the song Eternal Flame – The Bangles and used to play it full tilt most days her husband was up on border. Think me and my mum knew all of the words after the first six weeks!!! Too sexy – Right Said Fred was in the charts and much more. Alan went up to the border and lent me his stack stereo with a CD player, compact discs had been around a while but not as a general thing, vinyl records were still sold and cassettes, by around 1988 they were being sold alongside these. I was suitably impressed although didn't own a single CD, Alan had Purple Rain – Prince and the Revolutions Album. It was great having such a piece of modern technology in my bedroom.

Alans dad worked in Dharan International Airport, Saudi Arabia. 2nd August 1990 Iraq launched their invasion of Kuwait kicking off the Gulf War; it was to last until March 17th 1991. It was a very worrying time and with communications not being their best letters or phone calls were gratefully received.

We married 5th October 1991, Alans dad, Great Auntie Dot and Great Uncle Ron and Dean Draycott (my cousin), my parents and David being the only family members in attendance. We moved into our first married quarter, a two bed-roomed ground floor flat, this being my 20th home. Everything we needed from a tin opener to carpets was fully supplied, although we bought all our own and had many a wedding present of silk or satin sheets too. I was asked by Alan what we'd like in the way of furniture as a wedding gift from his dad, I'd replied a small decent corner television unit or an oval coffee table. When we moved into the flat I found a near six foot long television unit and a rectangle coffee table. Military coffee tables were rectangles and I never wanted the same, I also knew houses in the UK came a lot smaller than abroad hence asking for a corner unit for the television. The fact we'd got both was a bonus but we had some fun post Hong Kong with the size of said presents.

Alan had his own computer which was pretty impressive considering the size and cost of them. We'd had computers in school from around 1984 and home computing took off steadily from there on in. We took a trip and bought a stand for it to go in our bedroom and couldn't stop laughing when we found the instructions for our flat pack were in some weird and wonderful language. He wouldn't give up and managed through the pictures logically put it together. One of the first of many flat packs that we'd embark upon building.

For our honeymoon we went to Phuket in Thailand. I've never seen anything like it outside of a film. I remember watching Blue Hawaii (an Elvis Presley film) with my mum once and looking out of the window I was totally in awe. The most beautiful beaches, idyllic settings, people so friendly and hard working. We had a baby elephant at our hotel, just used to roam around with its' keeper, very cute but I'm sure not right for the elephant. We went to watch elephants at work and got to ride on one in a seated basket type thing, we also saw traditional dancing, it was a really lovely time, rode on a tuk-tuk which was mental, they're like motorised rick shaws/taxis. It was also the first time I'd flown without my parents and the first time I'd flown in a 'little' plane, very narrow island hopper.

We loved it so much we took David there the following year as a last minute deal leaving the day before my parents came back from holiday in Bali. We hired a jeep for a couple of days and went proper exploring, we found a sort of zoo/park with various monkeys/apes, crocodile/alligator and elephants, one of which would stood outside as the place wasn't quite open yet after lunch. The guy sort of holding the elephant motioned for us to go over and he nodded up at the elephants head indicating David could go on up. Sat on the elephants head David promptly squealed that the hairs were to spikey and were sticking in him. Later during the holiday we had a proper ride in basket seats. Alan and David shared a jet ski, Davids life vest being far too big and making him look like a turtle, great times.

When it came to leave Hong Kong having worked for the Royal Hong Kong Police and been made redundant as it were I had been offered the opportunity to cruise back to the UK on the QE2, because I was married and six weeks off giving birth to my second child I declined the offer. The 13 hour flight was quite the experience with a five year old and my being heavily pregnant. We left in November 1992.

We had removals for our furniture, we'd recently bought a dining table with six chairs and a stereo cabinet, lamp table and drum stool the same number one colour rosewood as the tv cabinet and coffee table but anything we wanted to pack ourselves was good old wooden MFO boxes, so there we were on the balcony of our ground floor flat screwing up boxes and over filling them, I remember thinking to myself how they thought we'd ever be able to weigh them. I do know that everyone and anyone was involved in a unit move so boxes were humped and dumped by all able bodied humans. Oddly enough when you packed yourself very few things were broken and it was actually quite a good laugh packing up. David kissed his grandparents goodbye and off we went.

Chapter 7

Home count stands at 21, Tern Hill, Shropshire, November 1992. We were literally an hour away from my grandparents; I was so excited to have them so close and couldn't wait for them to meet my husband. We hired a car and went as soon as we could. The house itself had red carpets downstairs and magnolia walls and beige curtains. The living room looked like someone had thrown up a trifle. First thing we did was paint it white with a hint of pink, it was woodchip paper on the walls so we'd been told any improvements would be fine. Metal framed windows were a nightmare to clean. We had a military three piece suit and it was hideous, it really did hurt my back sitting on it and we quickly discovered the local DFS and got a suite ordered.

My parents were still in Hong Kong and my brother in Chepstow area somewhere. My friend Julie Vidler was getting married and asked if I would be matron of honour and photographer. I was so happy to do so and laughed a lot when people at the wedding decided I couldn't be 32 weeks pregnant and someone must have made a mistake, seemingly I was too neat.

We also had a coal fire which our central heating ran off. Off we went to the local market and bought a hearth rug. I went off to get my hair cut before baby was born and came back to Alan sat on the edge of sofa looking worried. I said "don't tell me the fridge freezer hasn't arrived", "no, lift the hearth rug up" I did so and saw a huge black mark. Top tip for future reference, don't empty hot ashes into a cardboard box onto a brand new fitted carpet having moved your new hearth rug, then sweep it up with a plastic dustpan and brush. I couldn't stop laughing.

Alans days were spent humping and dumping MFO boxes to various houses and sorting out the equipment coming back from Hong Kong. We were contacted by the port authorities saying that we'd have to pay tax on our rosewood furniture as it was less than six months old when it had been packed up to come back to the UK. I was really angry when the stuff eventually arrived at our house to find two of the chairs had legs come off thanks to the fact they had been unpacked and repacked by the customs people. Never have had them repaired!! Getting all our furniture into the house was really quite funny but having a dining room made it easier. The long tv unit just fitted (phew).

Christmas was spent at my grandparents, it was so warm and so lovely, on Christmas Eve my cousin and his girlfriend came round and a few others, we were all laughing and joking when I spotted an advert out of the corner of my eye, it looked like a milking machine of some description but it was actually a condom testing machine with a Mrs Dawson being a condom tester, I couldn't stop laughing and it was pretty much decided I would have the baby there and then through laughing. My granddad an incredibly quiet gentleman smiled as the laughter had settled and told us a story of how they used 'french letters' to keep their weapons dry in the war. My cousins wife was utterly jaw dropped I don't think she'd ever heard more than a hello from him. Sam Richard Wansboro arrived on Wednesday 30th December 1992 at 9.03pm at North Staffordshire Hospital, Stoke-on-Trent.

Tern Hill was an unremarkable place; my parents came over with the rest of the regiment in January of 1993 and lived about a mile away over the main road. They brought my grandparents to meet Sam and it was the same feeling over again when my granddad held him in his arms and just beamed. David started the local primary school and went by bus daily. It didn't sit well with me that my five year old little boy was going to school by himself on a bus, but then my parents had waved us off many a time. He loved Sam and was very proud of his little brother. We had sort legal advice and been informed that we had to be married at least one year before we could adopt David, there was no step-parent adoption at that point, I would have to adopt my own flesh and blood weirdly. The adoption went through after Glenys

Williams (Davids Nain) had told her son to do the right thing and sign the paperwork.

6th April 1992 the Adjutant General's Corps was formed an amalgamation of the Army Legal Corps, the Corps of Royal Military Police, the Military Provost Staff Corps, Royal Army Educational Corps, Royal Army Pay Corps, Womens Royal Army Corps and all Staff Clerks from the Royal Army Ordnance Corps. I won't go into the whole history of it all but in April or May 1993 Alan was told as a Military Clerk within the regiment he would have to decide between redundancy or becoming AGC (SPS) getting almost instant promotion to Lance Corporal. Infantry were paid more so it was really to avoid loss of earnings.

Kenny moved back home with my parents and worked in the local Muller factory, making a great friend in Glynn Harrhy, they were practically joined at the hip at one stage. I decided I too would get a job and applied at the local pizza/pie manufacturing company Palethorps. Mum had agreed to look after the children once I'd got the job. I had never worked in a factory and the lady who interviewed and gave me the job warned it wasn't for me but I was annoyed at being judged and gave it a go. I should have listened she was so right, in my entire life I'd never heard stories and language like it, I lasted all of eight hours and never went back.

November 1993 we'd gone to see my grandparents and my Nan said to me in the kitchen "have a word with your granddad he's not eating well, he's got a problem swallowing and won't go to the doctors". My granddad was quite proud of being able to pull his belt in a couple of notches but she was right he did look a bit on the slim side. I mentioned that a few years before I'd had an issue with bread and eating if I was full of wind and very hungry, I'd had investigations and it was nothing more than a touch of stress and indigestion. My granddad agreed to go and see the doctor and not long after was diagnosed with stomach cancer. We went to stay with my parents in Chepstow for Christmas, dad had been made redundant earlier in the year and they'd moved back to their home. We went to see my granddparents on Boxing day; Granddad had tried to stay up for as long as possible but was very worn out. We had to go back to Tern Hill on

December 30th and realised it was Sams 1st birthday, I don't remember if we celebrated or not. Alan had to go off for Northern Ireland training and whilst he was away I had a phone call from my mum saying I needed to cone and say goodbye as Granddad was calling the nurse Julie. I got a taxi and train leaving my sons with Sarah Groves and Vanessa Conner and cried my heart out all the way there. I got a taxi from the station as I didn't want to risk my dad not being there with my mum if granddad died whilst he was coming to get me. The last words my Granddad said to me were "no germs" as I had an almighty sneeze sat in the chair next to his bed. I don't remember where I slept or how long I stayed, I did go home and January 22nd 1994 I got the call to say that the most wonderful true gentleman, my Granddad had died. I loved him with all my heart and knew he loved me unconditionally.

I borrowed some decent black clothing from Sarah Groves a good friend who lived across the way from us. It was agreed (by whom I couldn't tell you) that it wasn't appropriate for a six and one year old to go to a funeral, this would mean that I would be alone at the funeral. We all went to the house beforehand, Alan, David and Sam stayed in the living room as I slipped up into the bathroom to get changed into my borrowed clothes. I'd tried to arrange for the family to get together and have the word Granddad spelt out in flowers to no avail; seemingly there was an argument about how much each family would have to pay, ridiculous!! I went to our local florist and had a heart shaped small wreath made with the word Granddad in small flowers on it.

Everyone it seems was invited to go and see Granddad that morning or the night before I really don't remember, I had been told it wasn't a good idea for me to go and see him. Again, something decided for me not by me. The car arrived and as soon as I saw the coffin the tears started and I don't think they really stopped that day until we were back in the house and I was cuddling up to my sons.

Hereford was 'home' for me all my life until that point, it didn't matter how many houses I lived in, Brampton Road was home.

Chapter 8

Our last posting as part of the mobile village was to be to Ballykelly, Northern Ireland. This was also our last wooden MFO box move. I'd first lived in Northern Ireland 1973-1975. We were doing a direct swop with the Welsh Guards; I bumped into a few familiar faces during that move, one of whom was Jonah Jones who informed that they ('the corps of drums') had known why I left and were pleased I had. The house in Ballykelly is possibly the dirtiest house I've ever had the misfortune to move into. It was stinking and I vowed I'd never scrub another house after that.

I should explain. You have what used to be called a 'march in' and 'march out' procedure whereby members of the families' office and estate wardens department would make sure your house was absolutely spotless and damage free. It was the worst experience of the whole moving process and would send women of all ages and dispositions into terror and flat spins. Inspectors were known to don white gloves and trail fingers above door frames and beneath cooker grills and God forbid so much as a spec of dirt landed on those gloves. If your carpet was stained you were billed, if there was any damage you were billed, in short the house had to appear practically unlived in no matter how long you'd lived in it. Even down to losing keys, you'd be charged for a whole new lock etc. I'd scrubbed my house in Tern Hill and the woman who was moving in was over the moon ecstatic it was so clean. Then I moved into that squalor in Ballykelly, I was so angry.

I got a job in the Army Education Centre as assistant to the Chief Clerk. It was as part of a scheme and paid all of £26 a week but I loved it. Betty McNerlin, she was a member of the civil service and an awesome person to work for, she encouraged me to take more exams in word processing and typewriting to improve my curriculum vitae. She also encouraged me to apply for teaching evening classes in word processing and keyboard skills which I did and taught a six week course. It was a great wage booster.

Chloe Williams married Rob McKillop and we invited them over to stay for Christmas that year, they nervously accepted. I had no idea why they were so worried sounding and once they arrived they

50

were fine in the house; then I said I needed to go into town. Both visibly blanched, so I asked what's wrong, it did make me chuckle, they were expecting something like an old school street stand-off with Protestants down one side and Catholics down the other. Once we got into town they didn't relax but thankfully enjoyed Christmas at our home. Ballykelly was a moment where after we'd unpacked everything we'd found our Christmas tree was missing, hot footing it to the local supermarket to get another. We think it's still in the attic in Tern Hill. I hadn't realised how the 'troubles' looked to the rest of the world and the UK. To me it was just something we lived around things had seemed to calm down a lot with less bombings on the mainland and fewer shootings.

Alan would spend six or so weeks up at the various check points in Northern Ireland and home for four. One day he came home and said a camp dog named Tripod had a litter of seven puppies by one of the officers dogs that had been up on check points. He suggested we have one, I said outright no way as we were both working David and Sam were growing up fast and I didn't particularly want any more ties. I got a phone call at work maybe a week later and low and behold a puppy was waiting for us in one of his friends houses. We went from work to pick her up, a ball of white fluff, shaking like a leaf, no idea when last fed, walked or had pooped. We took her straight to the vet who gave her a worming tablet and all her necessary injections, then into town to pick up something for her to eat and something for her to eat out of., whilst in the car park she threw up the biggest round worm I've ever seen in the history of worms, it was disgusting to say the very least.   An egg banjo is given it's name as invariably when you eat a fried egg roll the yolk manages to drip out and whilst you hold it in one hand you try and capture the yolk with the other thus looking like you're playing a banjo, the pup had been fed on such by the lads on camp and so she was named Banjo, a Jack Russell, Springer Spaniel cross.

Kenny was now living up in Wakefield and was seeing a lass named Heather; seemingly she worked for River Island. We met Heather in Chepstow whilst visiting my parents on a couple of occasions and we all really liked her. Heather gave birth to Abbie Kaye Page Downs on 13th August 1995 and they moved into a council house in Wakefield not far from Heathers mum. Handy really that Banjo and Abbie were born in the same year; I had no problems remembering how old she was going to be on her birthday, hehehe!!

I read a lot of books from the library whilst in Ballykelly one being the complete history behind the 'troubles'. I advise anyone to research this subject as it'll give a vast insight into British and United Kingdom mentality toward their own. The 'troubles' have never really had anything to do with religion it was more about land ownership with things coming to a head when the Catholic Pope backed the people Ireland against the wishes of the Protestant mainland, now it's just an excuse as far as I can see. My parents were uneasy about our being in NI but agreed to come over for Christmas in 1995.

Our first experience of a full pack with a proper removals company coming in to pack up absolutely everything and deliver it to your next house, it was quite odd. Lisburn, Northern Ireland, having been assured we wouldn't move before Christmas my parents and Nan had arranged everything, only for us to move on the 21st and have my parents come to the new place in Lisburn. It was bleak, thick snow and treacherous ice meant I don't think we met any neighbours till about June!! My mum was poorly and had to go into the local hospital to say I was worried is an understatement, I had no idea what the protocol was for visiting etc. Thankfully it was a short stay and she was able to be at ours for Christmas.

I got a job working for the Army Families Federation as office manager in September 1996. I soon found out a lot more about the Army and it's slow but sure modernising attitude toward families. A young wife came into the office one day in floods of tears, she had been informed she could but nothing on her walls. Turns out her house had been replastered and was to settle, I went around the corner to see the Lt. Col in charge of such things to ask him if the information she'd been given was correct. The lady was indeed allowed to put things on the wall as long as said 'things' were on proper picture hooks, no nails, blutack etc. I also found out that day that from here on in houses would be painted magnolia with fitted carpets replacing any of the very very old school squares of carpet that used sit in the middle of the floor with a nice 60cms of tile showing. No more blue bedrooms when your children were girls and you wanted pink or vice versa, bright yellow kitchens that if clean deemed fine. Since being married I'd not had a quarter without fitted carpets, though Hong Kong had parquet floors. The job was on camp and in order to get onto camp you had an Identity Card, in order to work in some of the areas you were also vetted and given a second pass to gain entry to them. Alan worked inside a camp inside the camp this area was named HQNI.

October 7th 1996, we'd returned from the mainland and my parents new home in Brecon, South Wales after spending half term and our wedding anniversary there. A friend took me shopping as my husband went into work, I was just getting the last item (some boot laces) when there was the most enormous bang, sounded like the ceiling had come in at the supermarket. The assistant who'd shown me to the laces and I looked at each other, I said "is that what I think it was?" she just nodded.

I got my goods to the till as soon as I could and listened to the girl twittering over and over 'it's my mammys' birthday the day', then a young lad squeaking 'it's HQNI, it's HQNI' was rushing back in forth at the end of the tills, Kev Palmer appeared at the end of the till and said 'we've got to go now'. I had nothing in the house and said to Kev I had to get this shopping home, so the food flew through the check out and into bags, all sort of slow motion after that, packing up the shopping, leaving my eggs on top of the cheque signing bit, out into the car park and Kev checked under the car not two seconds later the second blast went off, everyone in the car park either ducked down or hit the floor; I stood silently watching the plumes of black smoke. There was no way they were going to let us into camp, I knew then how my mother had felt during the bomb scare she'd experienced all those years before, only the evidence of an actual exploded bomb was there right in front of my eyes.

After getting home I got the children and went straight back to the house trying to keep everything normal as humanly possible, both Carolyn and Kev practically begging me to stay with them. I heard nothing from my husband for hours, I'd fed and bathed the kids and put them to bed, my father-in-law rung from Saudi but I had nothing to tell him, he hadn't left a number for me to call back on and I was trying to

53

find out from the operator if they could tell me the number he'd called from to no avail. Then having just put the phone down Carolyn Palmer rang the doorbell bringing me some cigarettes she said "he's alright he's just rung mine as you were engaged". I think it was after I closed the door I cried. It was and remains one of the weirdest moments of my life. The news had said casualties had been taken to the medical centre, the second bomb had gone off just down from there killing a 41 year old soldier in his last six months of service. Those hours flew past and yet seemed endlessly slow. I've never discussed with my sons how they felt on that day, maybe one day I should or who knows they too might write their memoirs. Lisburn was remembered for all the wrong reasons.

I went and signed up with a temping agency and started working for Walkers Windows a family run double glazing firm. The daughter-in-law was taking maternity leave and was responsible for all the computer accounts along with all the book keeping. It was odd not telling them anything about myself but that was a no, no, you didn't say 'mess', 'awol' you avoided all military sounding words and NEVER discussed your spouses place of work. Having really only ever worked in military establishments or on the mainland where it didn't really matter what you said as long as you physically didn't give someone a map of a military establishment and say 'hey the best way in and to plant a bomb is...' etc. and having been military my entire life I had to think about stuff I said before saying it.

My father-in-law came to visit in January 1997, the first time we'd seen him since the wedding. He was calling in either before or after a hospital visit on the mainland, we thought for a back operation but he also had a lump removed from his throat. This was his first meeting of Sam a happy four year old with a dark mop of curly hair. We got new that we were posted to Cyprus to Ayios Nikolaos to be precise. I knew this was nowhere near the coast and the time had come to learn to drive if I were to have any chance of enjoying the posting. I failed my test first time around and having watched the 'packers' pack up all our stuff we hot footed it to my parents home in Brecon for a short break before our flights. Ay Nik being inland we felt it would be far too hot for Banjo and my parents agree to take care of her whilst we were posted out there, their first experience of having a dog since

54

they'd been married. I went out with a driving instructor for an hours lesson, he told me there was nothing he could teach me and he'd keep an eye out for a test cancellation he could slot me into. I wasn't confident so when he did ring and say you've got a date for a test in Newport I politely declined, I'd take my test in Cyprus.

The removal men, well that was an experience. They were to pack up two different lots of stuff, one for storage and one to come with us to Cyprus. I'd been in work for most of the packing up, the boxes I'd packed for storage had a list to go inside and a list for us to keep, I got home to find that all said lists were sat altogether so I never did know exactly what we were leaving behind.

Whilst at my parents Alan found out his dad had cancer, it was to be treated, I asked Alan if he wanted to try for a compassionate posting within the UK so that he could support his aunt and extended family whilst his father received treatment. For reasons only Alan will know he chose to continue with our posting to Cyprus. Alan went to visit his dad who gave him his video camera. It was a huge thing that looked a lot like television cameras only a bit smaller. We made various little films over the summer of the boys and said we'd send a video as often as possible after our arrival in Cyprus.

When we arrived in Cyprus it was like a wall of heat had just smacked us in the face, it was July and absolutely boiling. We were the second occupants of a new build; civilians working for the MOD had lived in it previously and as we were not entitled to air conditioning there were some beautiful marks on the wall where it had once lived. The removals arrived and we duly started unpacking and to everyone's horror we found the television had gone into storage!!! I also remembered leaving our game of Monopoly on top of a cupboard in the kitchen, ho hum! It was difficult to get a telephone they said up to six weeks, we pleaded our case as we had Alan senior receiving cancer treatment but to no avail.

Ayios Nikolaos was to be Sams first day at school, grey shorts and white shirt, exactly the same as Davids first uniform back in Hong Kong. We took videos of the house, Sams first day at school, Ay Nik in general and started to settle into life in a hot climate. We met Sarah,

Natalie and Amy Lowe that first day at school, Sarah married to big tall Pete and Natalie same age as Sam but head and shoulders taller bless her. Natalie and Sam became great friends and went to each others birthday parties, then they moved down to Episkopi and we lost touch a bit.

A neighbour let me use their phone to check on things at home and also said anyone could call them in case of an emergency. I met Donna Wood and her two sons Connor and Liam and hubby Woody a chef. 31st August 1997 Donna and I were out in our gardens pegging out washing and she called over 'put the news on Princess Dis dead', thinking no way I came indoors to call up "Alan, Princess Di's dead" I put the tele on and there it was all over the news. Alan came downstairs his face ashen and was about to ask something then looked at the television. Years later he told me he thought I'd shouted up "Alan your dads dead".

Sadly in September a knock at the door revealed a soldier in uniform asking to come in and for Alan to sit down, his father had died of pneumonia during his cancer treatment. The military has this really weird thing where if someone is dying or going for a life threatening operation you are considered Cat A compassionate case, if they're already dead you're not a priority. They did fly Alan back for the funeral, this may sound weird but the children and I weren't welcome by Alans family to go and see my father in law before he died and weren't welcome at the funeral. Another to this day I don't know why, I was upset at not being able to be by his side to support him through his grief, I hadn't been able to when his mother died as we were just 'seeing' each other at that time.

Alans father left quite a large inheritance and during the rest of the year this was all to be sorted out; Alan wanted to have a Land Rover Freelander a new car developed by the group (late 1997) to lock into the SUV market. Knowing that the first part of the inheritance would be available fairly quickly Alan duly placed his order. The vehicle was to prove a bit of a nightmare and it was rapidly replaced with a three door Freelander with removable roof, we all loved it, driving down to Aya Napa music blasting sun kissed faces enjoying the wind in our faces; David and Sam cringing when I'd sing along loudly.

56

News came in Ayios Nikoloas that my Uncle Trefor was diagnosed with pancreatic cancer, it was untreatable and therefore terminal, it was a matter of time. He sold up from the area he'd been living and went to live by the coast, having been an avid diver all his life it made sense. Clearly not wanting to admit defeat from the off the illness he contracted whilst his immune system was weakened were treated so he had many a trip to hospital, in the end having to stay in. Kenny witnessed the vile deterioration of Uncle Trefor, going from a hulk of a man to a yellow stick thin shadow. Uncle Trefor died on his wedding anniversary nearly two years after his diagnosis.

I had a job with the RAF in Ay Nik and it was a real eye opener. The attitude in the RAF was very different. Their postings were mainly in the UK as most RAF bases were closing or closed in Germany. Many seemed to buy their own homes almost within days of joining up and when married as their postings were usually all in the UK they would commute. Met a navy lad in Ay Nik too, he too explained that in the Navy the families tended to live in one place in their own homes and the 'men' would go sea. Navy could spend anything up to a year at sea, RAF it seems would only ever be away for four months or so, with the Army generally doing six month tours.

In January 1999 we moved to Episkopi, back to the coast, we'd gone back to the UK for Christmas and picked Banjo up and brought her over, it was mad, just like the first time I'd lived there nothing seemed to have changed at all. The Lowes lived a few streets down so that friendship was recaptured.

Summer 1999 we spent sometime in the UK and went to the Bristol Balloon Festival. As part of my mums birthday present I paid for us to go up in a helicopter. We could see everything, all of the balloons getting ready, the whole of the fair ground, it makes me laugh remembering this experience, when I was thinking about a career I'd like to pursuit when I left school I'd thought of becoming the first female helicopter pilot for the British Army, just as well that didn't happen, the views were great but oh my word not something I'd repeat in a hurry.

We had a wicked street party for the millennium and sure did party like it was 1999. For my 30th birthday present we went to Egypt. It was a whistle stop trip taking in the pyramids, Sphinx and the museum. We even went inside a pyramid. An utterly amazing trip, seeing Tutankhamen's' treasures was something I'll always be amazed by. I don't do well on boats so the crossing from Cyprus to Egypt wasn't the best but the day trip seeing all of that more than made up for it.

I was now in my 25th home, my 6th married home, I was working for the RAF and both children were in school. My eldest in St Johns, the school I had attended aged 12-14, one of my old teachers was still there!! Being in Episkopi had felt like 'going home' it was quite bizarre at first, it was fun showing the children all the places I remembered so fondly. My father-in-law had left quite a substantial inheritance and we had a good life, both having new cars and buying my Nans house in Hereford.

The World Rally had come to Cyprus in 2000 and off we went to find and watch it, David was really into cars and as it was a Cyprus first and on our doorstep it was a must. We met Nicky Grist and saw Colin McCrae who was in 'the zone' and didn't want to be fussed or have pictures taken which is fair enough. Nicky Grist however was more than happy to chat and answer every question an awe struck David could ask.

My parents and Nan came over and we all retraced our footsteps of 1982-1984, visiting our old house in Gibraltar village and sitting on the viewpoint sharing memories of my granddad and our life there. It was quite funny when we got our next posting, we were off to Germany, history repeating.

March 2001 and a move to Gutersloh, Germany, it was freezing! I got a job pretty quickly and gave it up just as quickly, I thought about retraining. We spent the whole of the summer that year in the UK at my parents. Part of Alans' inheritance were stocks and shares, we didn't really understand them so decided to sell them all. We used the money to put double glazing in Brampton Road and for a tenth wedding anniversary present – a trip to New York, USA. August

2011, our flight took us to Amsterdam where we were to change plane and flew into JFK.

A show on Broadway A Thousand Clowns starring Tom Selleck, every landmark you could think of, you name it we did it, venturing up The World Trade Centre Tower 2 on the 13th August, ONE HUNDRED AND EIGHT storeys up. It was such a cloudy day but a couple offered to take our picture for us so at least we had the record of the visit. I bought a t-shirt with the observation deck on it.

Having returned to Germany in September 2001 and showing the photos to all my friends it was an unreal moment when my friend called across the garden to turn the television on (bringing back memories of Donna calling over in Cyprus). An aeroplane had deliberately crashed into one of the twin towers and moments later a second one had crashed into the other, I sat open mouthed unable to take in what I was witnessing. The day became known as 9/11, 911 being the emergency services number in the USA. The single worse terrorist attack anywhere in the world and a blow to the USA of incomparable consequence, only Peal Harbour had seen such an attack to mainland USA. The consequences have been world and life changing for many.

Gutersloh was a pretty town in parts, it was rumoured that the place was built on a swamp and Hitler refused to put troops there as the sickness rates were so bad. There was a lot of asthma and pneumonia there amongst military families, so who knows the rumours might have been true. Personally I had Bells Palsy in September 2001 and was in hospital when the memorial services and vigils were held for the victims and families of the 9/11 terror attack. After that stay I was incredibly surprised to fall pregnant!

Alan and I had decided to take ante-natal classes before number 3 was born; it was here we met Kim and Iain Wallace. Iain was well into all the gore of child birth none of the videos we watched phased him. Their child was due in the May as ours was due in the June. Nicola Wallace was born 27th May 2002 and Rebecca Drew Wansboro born 20th June 2002 in Bielefeld in a German hospital; all the military hospitals in Germany had closed by that time as had all the ones in the UK too. Kim and Iain went on to become the closest thing to aunties and uncles along with Chloe and Rob that my children have.

In October 2002, my parents, Kenny and Abbie (he'd split with Heather by then) and us went to Disneyland Paris for my nieces 8th birthday. It's funny right up until I had my first child my dad had promised to take us to Disneyland (the one in the USA) and we never got there, so we all went then. We didn't see anything of Paris itself and didn't venture out of the park, it was a brilliant holiday.

Alan went to Kosovo in January 2003 for six months, the first six month tour Alan had done, David was 15 and Sam 10, Rebecca at six months was developing at a normal rate and it worried me Alan would miss so much. When you have a six month tour you have two weeks rest and recuperation, where possible people take it in the middle but obviously that would be impossible for everyone to do. Alan arranged to take his R&R around Rebeccas 1st birthday.

I met one of my closest ever friends in Gutersloh, Louby Lou, Louise Philips. One day my door was knocked and friends said "come and see the state of your car", I rolled my eyes and said "really?" Out I went to see that my Vauxhall Astra looked as if someone had taken a giant tin opener to the boot right below the spoiler. Literally as we were inspecting the damage a tall fella came over and said "Hi I'm Dick, this was my fault", I thought yes you are aren't you!! The start of a long and beautiful friendship with the family consisting of Louby, Rich, Jake and Aiden and their dog Guinness a gorgeous black Labrador, they had moved into the last house of our terrace. During Alans R&R I fell pregnant and not long after I found out Louby told me she was three months pregnant. Alan returned from Kosovo in the July and Louby and I grew fat together.

Christmas 2003 my dad decided it was about time life was spiced up a little and had a heart attack. January 2004 saw me thirty odd weeks pregnant and flying over to the UK with my what 19 month old daughter. After a few false starts and much worry dad had a double bypass, he was out of hospital and on his road to a full recovery before I returned to Germany. I wanted to be in the UK with my parents as I'm not sure I could have coped being in Germany unable to see them and just getting phone call updates. Mum, Rebecca and me went back and forth daily to Cardiff a three hour round trip, the parking cost a bloody fortune. Everyone was so lovely to us all, they really cared and true friendships shone through, each evening my poor mum would be on the phone repeating the days events over and over to various concerned friends and family returning missed calls etc. My brother managed to really annoy me by visiting our father only once and then for an extremely short length of time, all dads family covering for Kenny saying "oh he couldn't see his dad like that it upset him", really? What exactly did he think it was doing to my mum and the rest of us?

Once dad was out of hospital and given the all clear I returned to Germany and met Elena better known as Ellie belly biscuit to me, Lou had given birth in the corridor at the hospital whilst I'd been in the UK. I did chuckle only Lou! I went for my final check up with my bump being a day overdue, I was not impressed. Coming home that afternoon I was pretty fed up, then a twitch and a bit of an ache and I thought I'd best get to hospital. Louby took Rebecca for me and David and Sam took care of themselves and off Alan and I went back to the Gilead. Eve Louise Wansboro, Monday 15th March 2004 at 8.41pm was born in the same room as Rebecca with the same midwife!

Alan was threatened with an eight month tour of The Falkland Islands, to leave in the July, for the first time ever I said NO!! If I was to stay in Gutersloh we needed a bigger house. I was advised to go through the Army Welfare Service and plead my case, I'd never involved the 'families office' or 'welfare centres' in any of my army life and I didn't relish the idea of having to do so now but for my own sanity went down the various routes. If we had been in the UK and this was a council house procedure it would have been straight forward, when there is a five year age gap between your children they are advised to have their own room, this meant for us David having his own room, Sam having his own room and our daughters sharing. This meant the need for a four bed roomed house.

In the meantime Alan was arguing and fighting his corner not to be posted to the Falklands, there was no way on this planet was I being stuck with a new born baby, a two year old and the threat of moving house alone!!! I saw the CPN the AWS and all to no avail

61

there was no way they were going to move us into a four bed. I was incredulous. Thankfully Alan managed to secure a job within Germany and a move loamed.

June 2004 David moved to the UK to stay with my parents until he was due to start boarding college there are no further education facilities in service schools other than straight forward A level or NVQ courses, David was to go for a mechanics course in Chichester in the September, he'd passed all of his GCSEs, as a reward we paid for his trip to Spain where he stayed with his friends family at their caravan.

In August with Eve being four months old we moved to Monchengladbach. Nothing was worth talking about in this place. There was an autobahn at the end of our enormous, mole ridden garden and the area itself was flat and featureless. The saving grace of Monchengladbach was the friends I made there. A thriving and lively parent and toddler group which saved my sanity. Helen Whitehead was the organiser she had two little girls close in age to mine, her youngest at the time was Meg, an absolute star of a child who regularly stripped off anywhere and everywhere. When over to play one afternoon in the summer we were out in the garden and turned to see Meg not a stitch of clothing but a lovely pair of clip clop sparkly shoes and some Pat Butcher earrings lent up against the doorframe we couldn't stop laughing (sorry Meg we did take your picture after you'd put your knickers on at the very least). Kim and Iain came to visit and we visited them, a tradition started of spending New Years Eve together. One year the people across the road were being somewhat reckless with fireworks and Kim marched over and told them straight to pack it in; turned out he was the Royal Military Police and their WO2 too!! I did however have my appendix removed in the local hospital in 2005 (waking to be told in fact I have endometriosis and my appendix was healthy). My parents came over to help and my mum and I finally had the conversation about children, it seems I was never meant to be the last child, they'd wanted a big family and it had just never happened. When my mum had a hysterectomy years before they found she had endometriosis, this appeared to be the reason why after me there were no more.

Sam broke his wrist when a major football match was taking place, my husband had issues getting him to the hospital until a police man saw it and helped him leave the estate!!!

Chapter 9

In January 2006 we moved to Uxbridge, a suburb of London. My 28th home, David number one sons 15th home, Sam number two sons 8th home, and our daughters 3rd home both under the age of five!!! David moved back in with us in Uxbridge and started at the local college, Sam had to go to boarding school as the local Borough council didn't see a problem with his being out of school for months until they could find a place for him in a local school. Uxbridge was a total culture shock and I was grateful living behind the wire and in the safety of camp. The house was a little four bedroom terrace, really old with a bathroom without a window. I don't think I'd ever lived in a house where the bathroom didn't have a window, it was really weird and I didn't like it. Rebecca and Eve shared a room and had their own beds. My Nans 80th birthday was an event, we actually got her so drunk we had to carry her to bed, she got up the next day as bright as a button it was utterly hilarious. We went up to my parents in the August for my mums birthday and found my brother was there, the children were chuffed it was a great surprise.

Kenneth Francis Richard Draycott born 14th November 1968 was found dead in his flat on Wednesday October 11th 2006, we'd been back in the UK just over six months. I had a cake in the oven and another to go in once that one was out, I was looking after my friends daughter for a couple of hours and she and my girls were playing happily in the living room. The phone rang, my mum was hysterical crying "he's dead, he's dead", my first thought was my dad having had his heart by-pass two years previously, through heart wrenching sobs it became clear my brother was dead.

Alan was in work, David was in college, Sam was in boarding school, I just went numb and then sort of into over drive, made sure all the cakes for the following days parent and toddler group were finished, waited for my friend to pick up her daughter, rang Alan and rang David to come home, all I wanted to do was get to my parents.

Everything was just plain odd, I can't compare it to anything because I don't have the words. I went to my parents house, the facts were, Kenny last text on the Sunday night to Margaret his ex-girlfriend they were arguing about his being late to take the dogs out, he didn't then turn up for work on the Monday morning and Tuesday Margaret rang as someone from his work had rung her to see if she knew where he was, nobody had heard from him. Wednesday then the police and Margaret and Kennys mate/boss went to the flat and broke in. He was there dead in his bed, his clothes ironed and ready for work, mobile phone on charge, diary showing his appointments, all ready for when he was to get up. My dad was in work and Heather my nieces mum rang him. It was Heather not the police who told my dad, her brother had found out from someone and she'd rung to offer her condolences, my dad had to then drive home to tell my mum her son was dead. Seems one policeman never told or handed over to another policeman so the family liaison officer never made it to my parents home in Brecon, South Wales before news got out up in Wakefield, South Yorkshire.

I have absolutely no idea how my parents coped or cope with what happened. My parents and my son Sam went up to Wakefield to see Kenny, he was in Pinderfield Hospital. Seemingly he looked peaceful and as though he'd wake at any moment. The funeral was arranged, Alan, David, Sam, Rebecca, Eve and I all went to the funeral it was odd seeing two little girls dressed in black.

My parents had support, empathy and sympathy from the entire community and all of the regiment. Hundreds of cards, some letters and phone call after phone call, the funeral was held in Brecon Cathedral, I have no idea how many people came but it looked nearly full. Alan and Helen Harrhy, Barbara and Gary Gibbs, Sian and her husband, Wendy Floundes some of the people who hadmade the effort to come and support us all.; a convoy of cars snaked their way through the picturesque countryside to the crematorium, my Auntie Marion and Uncle Martin shared the car with us six, it was quite bizarre we hadn't had a great deal to do with them ever, not sure they could get their heads round our 'squaddie humour 'as a coping mechanism. We saw a rainbow and I told the girls Uncle Kenny had his first wee in heaven, that he was up there drinking beer (which for some reason became lemonade later) and eating crisps having a party. I found out later my mum had said he'd spent a penny too when the rainbow appeared.

When we got back to the house after the wake at the local RAFA club I took my parents dog for a walk accompanied by my 11 year old niece. We didn't talk much. I don't know when but Kennys ashes were ready to be picked up and we all went up the mountain near The Storey Arms to scatter them. All of my children throwing a handful to the wind and elements, I have to say he's got a bloody good view up there. That was the end. I've been up nearly every year around his birthday or whenever possible near the anniversary of his death just to say hello and have a think. I was so angry at him for not taking better care of himself and for hurting our parents so much and robbing my children of their Uncle!!!

The end for my parents was to go up to Wakefield to hear the coroners report in the January I think it was. They sat and listened to various accounts of the run up to his being found from his friends and his ex-girlfriend. The medical/science part concluded there was nothing of any significant amount in his body to have killed him so a verdict of death by misadventure was pronounced. It is widely believed he took a six weeks worth of prescription pain killers over two weeks thinking nothing of popping them like Smarties if the pain relief hadn't been instant, but as this was not given as cause we'll none of us ever really know.

One thing I do know and I don't care who agrees or disagrees my brother did not kill himself and had no intention of killing himself that night. There are several reasons why I know that to be fact not least the fact he'd put his phone on charge and not left a note to make sure whoever he blamed knew it was their fault!!

Very very slowly life settled into its' former routines though life would never be the same again. Visits to Brecon often as it combined ferrying Sam to and from boarding school in Leominster. Eventually we did do the whole London thing, but with two small children in tow it wasn't the most enjoyable day. We did the open top bus tour, went to all the landmarks although none of us wanted to wait for the London Eye. What can I say London is London; you either love it or hate it.

2007 saw the death of Colin McRae in a helicopter accident. It was shocking to think we'd seen him out in Cyprus that time. With his being one of David inspirations to take up car mechanics too.

I went to watch Puppetry of the Penis whilst living in Uxbridge, now that's a bizarre thing to watch in the theatre!!! Long and short of it, two men making shapes with their manhoods, you had to stop and think who did you ask what it looked like?

In 2008 we were posted to Brecon, Powys a stones throw from my parents' home. The Brecon Beacons National Park is an amazing place to live, its' scenery breath taking. Although unlike everyone else I've not managed to climb Pen y Fan. There is so very much to see in Wales, so many castles and history just seems to be everywhere. I'm very proud to be Welsh.

It was great having my parents up the road, Rebecca and Eve went to the school just down from their house so I'd go up in the morning with Banjo and join my mum walking Jack taking the girls to school. We could see as much or as little of each other as we wanted. Best times were ringing my mum and saying get your life sorted we're going out for the day, she'd ring my dad and say "oh we're off out, your lunch is in the bread bin". A trip on the canal boat, trip to Bristol zoo and the balloon festival, day trips to Barry Island, being able to go up to my nans for the day it was all good. In 2009 a new kitchen was put into 16 Brampton Road, what a bloody nightmare, from start to finish the company were rubbish, eventually calling in a private contractor who owned his own business to finish the work completely and properly, Nan and I had enough. We decided a break was in order so off we went to Verona, Italy to see my cousin Mathew and his girlfriend.

Verona with the balcony from Shakespeares Romeo and Juliet, the amphitheater where operas are performed regularly, the marble floors of the designer shops lined streets, everyone so chic and well heeled. Castel San Pietro overlooking Verona had superb views of the river and the oldest parts of the city and the Ponte Pietra or stone bridge completed in 100BC. The rich history tangible in most parts of the city. Mathew living in a modern flat on the outskirts drove us into town and down to Lake Garda where I'd spent my holiday back in 1984. We also went up to a little mountain village to watch Mathew in a road cycling race, it was brilliant, went into a cake shop/café and enjoyed some rather tastey treats.

16 Brampton Road was now different in many ways. Double glazing, central heating, walk in shower, new kitchen, new carpets, curtains, not sure my granddad would recognise the place anymore. The gardens still as beautiful as he had them, though his vegetable patch long gone with lawn replacing it, I hope he'd be happy that the house is still a home and still kept in the family.

Brecon Jazz festivals, meeting up with Nicola Mason (mouse) and Tracey Jones from Lemgo days, nights out with work colleagues and bizarrely Louby Lou and Rich moved in the other side of town just as our next posting was coming up. My closest friend in Brecon was my mum, it was a much needed posting close to home.

And so to house number 30, a three storey town house, brand new on a brand new estate in a brand new village in Gloucestershire. All I can say about that is someone needs to be given a good shake and told a few home truths about their design.

Originally back in the day military families were housed much in the same way as the council housed people. Purpose built homes so that families could live near their husbands' place of work. Each regiment then had a families office who would allocate a house appropriately, if you had two children a three bed-roomed house was available, four or more children a four bed-roomed house. This was not rank ranged in that you could only have the house you needed if you were a certain rank, however, most estates were laid out in such a way that you were close to people in the same age and rank range. The officers always had a separate patch and the RSM a detached four bed-roomed designated house. It worked; you tended to live near people with roughly the same amount of children and roughly the same age. The houses were big enough to store all your husbands' military kit and all your normal possessions. Houses in the UK were known to be on the small side but there was always space for a dining table. Houses in Germany were always bigger and you had both attic and cellar space, if you lived in a flat you'd still have a cage in the cellar where you could store all sorts. The families' office allocated you a house based on need and how many points you had, the estate wardens and families office 'marched' you in and out of your quarter and pretty much everything went to plan. Rarely was anyone told sorry we don't have a house for you.

Then in their infinite wisdom the whole lot was sold off to a management company namely Annington Homes and allocation for housing went from unit level to Housing Information Centres covering large areas. It was the single biggest mistake as far as looking after families went!!! Too many military built houses were sold off, leaving vast gaps in supply and demand causing a sway toward private hiring's costing far more than was necessary. The end result being, Annington Homes taking ten or more years leases on housing estates that had already been built without ever bothering to check location or suitability. You now have families living far from their spouses' place of work, possibly leaving a spouse unable to drive or only having one car, in an area with poor transport links. The cohesion of military life is being broken up and the big 'family' feeling has gone. The social aspects are also going fast as nobody wants to drive back into work for a function.

House number 30 proved to be the straw that broke the camels back. We had several very important visitors to our home all of which agreed it was totally unacceptable for a family of six to live in. The top man in all of this said and I quote "I will have you moved from here". True to his word six months later we moved, into a normal four bed-roomed two storey house, out of our entitlement as it's an officers' quarter and detached no less! This my 31st house is where I am now. Gloucester, with its' beautiful cathedral and long long history, the whole country is in recession and many shops and small businesses have closed. The high street looks pretty bleak at times and this estate is full of what they call 'affordable houses'. Eventually there'll be 3,000 houses here and I feel damned sorry for anyone who bought one. The military have realised that housing 100 of its' families here has failed and as soon as the contract is up nobody will be moved in, there are already some houses stood empty, one of which for the full two years we've been here.

My childhood with the army was fantastic, although I now know it was quite a ball of cotton wool I was wrapped in. Everyone I knew had a mum and dad, their dad had a job, everyone had a house to live in, nearly everyone had a car, the adults were all aged between 18 and 40, the only time you saw older people were visiting grandparents, every child got Christmas presents, even in Church Crookham when I went to the local primary then secondary school everyone seemed to have what they needed, but then I suppose I only really hung out with Chloe, there were very few ethnic soldiers other than the Ghurkhas, I think there was only one black man in my dads regiment and I remember when it was publically addressed that there weren't any ethnic soldiers in the Guards regiments. It took me a long time to learn about racism, sexism or any other ism for that matter. I didn't know that by its' very nature the army was in many ways everything ist!! Everyone had food and clothing, everyone went to school, nobody dared play truant and life was great. How on earth was I expected to know how it was for everyone else?

Clearly as an adult I can't claim ignorance and have had my eyes well and truly yanked open by the many varied and intrusive media mediums. It's all too clear that since time began there's been all sorts of everything going on in the world and I just never heard any of it when I was growing up.

Whilst living here Alan has done a tour of Afghanistan. In his infinite wisdom he had a heart attack whilst there. May 10th 2011 a phone call at 6pm saying "I won't be on Skype I'm on morphine in hospital" handing the phone back to his boss. May 11th 2011 saw him in Ramstein, Germany, May 12th having a stent fitted in the American hospital there, May 13th being visited by Angelina Jolie, oh and then me a bit later that day.

January 2012 saw him being told along with 1500 others that he was eligible for redundancy. The British military being so far over stretched and at war or United Nations peace keeping commitments around the world it's just a joke. Soldiers were invited to volunteer for redundancy. Alan is due to leave the army in 2015 having done 28 years by then. There was no point in his volunteering so didn't. In June 2012 the redundancies were announced my father Regiment is to be disbanded, gone for good!! Alan was not made redundant and we are to be posted to Germany.

The London Olympics 2012, soldiers coming back from tours of duty in Afghanistan many of whom face the disbandment of their regiments in the recent waves of cuts are proud and happy to act as security after a 57 million pound security cock up by a civilian security firm.

British Government please take note and learn your lessons. Management companies don't work when it comes to dealing with REAL people over paperwork and spreadsheets and pre tax profits.

The next house will be house number 32, we have not been allocated a room for my eldest son as he's too old to be living at home seemingly, nor have I been allocated a room for my second son as he's not in full time education and shouldn't be living at home seemingly, what exactly would the management company like me to do with my children, my family? The government have announced that benefits for under 25's are to be slashed or stopped, forcing people to either move back in with their parents or effectively become homeless, a round of applause please for their forward thinking. You can't nanny us one minute then tell us to grow up the next.

My dad retired March 31st having been made redundant for a second time with the MOD cuts and changes, he was working in a retired officers job for the civil service in the barracks in Brecon. My dad is 68 this year and my mum 65, they aren't too happy that we're leaving the country again, ironically my granddad was 68 and my Nan 64 when we went to Hong Kong, leaving Kenny in the UK, we're leaving David in the UK with my parents. My life thus far seems to have many interlocking circles of coincidence and right the way through people I've met continue to play a part.

The World Wide Web, the internet, the access to instant information has shrunk the world. There is no excuse for not keeping in touch or losing touch, however life and living can and does have habit of getting in the way. Whenever you meet up with a military friend it matters not when you last spoke as you always take up exactly where you left off. You'll rarely make truer friends.

The thought behind writing down all my experiences was to remember all the places I've seen, all the famous people I've met, all the things I've done, so that when I'm old and grey and the memories fade I can have a read and think WOW that was me!! It's not a history lesson so not every campaign and conflict in the world has been mentioned.

Rank Structure and approx numbers for a Regiment

Private	normally a couple of hundred
Lance Corporal	normally a couple of hundred
Corporal	normally a couple of hundred
Sergeant	25 – 30
Staff Sergeant	12
Warrant Officer Two	10
Warrant Officer One	1
2nd Lieutenant	12-14
Lieutenant	12-14
Captain	8-10
Major	8-10
Lieutenant Colonel	1

Printed in Great Britain
by Amazon

41184797R00046